MW00947397

B2B SALES

SECRETS

The Exact Step-by-Step Process
For Closing More Deals
From a Guy Who Generated
Over $30 Million in Sales

Eric Konovalov

As a bonus for purchasing this book, I'd like to thank you by giving you access to download some awesome resources.

Go to www.B2BSalesSecretsBook.com/BonusResources

And download your free:
√ Cold Calling Script
√ Sample Introduction Email Script
√ Daily Agenda Guide
√ What they buy vs. What we sell samples
√ Great Questions to Ask list

Thank you for your support. You're really going to enjoy this book!

-Eric

Contents

Acknowledgements

I would like to express my sincere gratitude to all the people who have developed me.

To Julia Konovalov, my wife, who supports me with all my crazy ideas and who loves me unconditionally.

To Max and Mikey, my children, who are the reason I strive to achieve my full potential.

To Veta Mesh, my mother, who has always allowed me to find my way and supported me in anything I ever tried.

To Larry and Irene Feldman, my in-laws, who make me feel like there is nothing I cannot accomplish.
To John Maxwell and everyone on The John Maxwell Team, for your mentorship, your support, and the lessons in personal development, which shaped me into the leader I am today.

To Patrick Johnson, the best consultative sales professional, friend, and mentor I could have ever asked for. Working with you as my mentor strengthened my desire to win.

To Vince Scarborough, President of DCA Imaging Systems, for giving me the opportunity to lead your sales department and for always including me in the high-level, strategic discussions.

To Dan Marchetti, Ginna Gallentine, and Jenny Bateman, the best sales professionals I've ever had the privilege and honor to work with. You make mc a better leader each day.

To Frank Curreri, my first sales manager, who taught me how to sell a copier in Baltimore and started me in my career in sales.

To Lieutenant Colonel Phillip "Joker" Welsh, one of the best Marines I've ever served with, for helping me realize that I was going to be great in the world of sales. Semper fi, sir!

Introduction

In 2006, when I was getting out of the marine corps, I went to my commanding officer, Lieutenant Colonel Welsh, and said, "Sir, I've been in the marines since I graduated from high school. What the hell am I going to do as a civilian?"

He looked back at me and said, "K (that was short for Staff Sergeant Konovalov), with all the bull crap you sold me through the years, you should get a job in sales!"

That's how I first heard of sales as a career. I immediately sent a résumé to anyone looking for sales reps and was invited for an interview by every Aflac location in the United States! I finally received and accepted an offer from an office-equipment dealership in Baltimore, Maryland, to sell copiers and other office equipment to local businesses. I remember sitting in a small office with my manager and him telling me to go cold-calling. I looked him right in the eye, and as serious as anything I've ever done, I asked, "What's cold-calling?"

Eager to learn everything the sales world had to offer, I quickly rose through the ranks and became one of the top salespeople in that company. Following my first sales job, I went on to sell medical devices to orthopedic trauma surgeons, manage a sales team for a Xerox company, and sell outsourcing services to international organizations, and for the last few years I've been enjoying developing salespeople as a director of sales at Digital Copier Associates (DCA).

At DCA, I found my purpose and passion. I realized my talent for helping people get to the next level of their lives by assisting them in getting unstuck and finding their purpose. I started the Goal Guide, Inc., a training-and-coaching company to help individuals and organizations excel at what they do and achieve the goals they've set for themselves. Whether it's C-level executives looking to improve the results of their companies, entrepreneurs who are looking for support in growing their businesses, sales professionals who want to grow their revenues, or people who are not where they want to be in life and are ready to make changes, the Goal Guide is there to help them get to the next level.

What I quickly realized is that people can be the very best in their professions or have the best products but that without the proper sales skills they're not able to effectively sell their services. I'm surrounded by amazing entrepreneurs who want to make our world a better place. They're excited to add value to other people's lives and bring products and services to the marketplace, but many of them fail because they don't have the proper sales skills to influence people to buy from them. This is the main reason I'm writing this book. It will give salespeople and entrepreneurs a road map to creating a successful buyer's journey, which will help them grow their businesses and revenues.

I coach and train business-to-business (B2B) sales professionals and often see the frustration they feel after getting rejected twenty times in a row. Or when a potential customer asks for an "emergency" proposal and disappears forever! Has that ever happened to you? I've seen way too many salespeople invest time and energy into building a relationship with someone for months or years and still lose a deal to a competitor.

I wish I could say that by reading this book you'll win all your sales opportunities, but that wouldn't be true. I don't want to come across as someone who wins them all; that isn't realistic. I think what differentiates me from most is that I decided to become a student of the trade. When I lost a deal, I wanted to know why. When I won a deal, I also wanted to know why. When it stalled or the client went dark, guess what? I wanted to know why! To improve my skills, I read books, listened to sales videos, attended seminars, and worked side by side with some of the best sales professionals in the country. I continue my learning habits today, and they've paid off big-time. My goal is to become the best I can be so that I can help you become the best you can be.

I'm writing this book for sales professionals, sales managers and leaders, CEOs, and entrepreneurs who want to increase their revenues and profit margins. It's also for organizational sales trainers who want a blueprint of a detailed sales process to take their new hires and veterans through. And it's for people who are fantastic at their professions and are interested in increasing their influence to grow their businesses. In this book, you will find a detailed three-part plan that will guide you from the initial contact with your potential clients to closing the sale and building long-lasting relationships. In part 1, we'll take a deep dive into how successful salespeople think and what they do differently to prepare for their success. In part 2, we create our buyer's journey. The buyer's journey is a map of our sales process. Once created, it will help you understand exactly where you are in the sales process, and it will effectively guide your clients to receive the best solution for them. The third part is where we learn about the most effective way to be after the sale. This is where you will create long-lasting relationships with your clients.

Being in sales is not easy. It may be the toughest profession to be in because most people hate rejection. It's tough to be hung up on, yelled at, and kicked out of office buildings and to approach people we don't know to try to convince them to buy a product or service that they may or may not need. The good news is that my sales approach is different. It provides sales professionals with ways to not only sell more of their products or services but also genuinely attract the client and develop a genuine relationship. As a matter of fact, if you follow my process, most of the people you reach out to will at least give you a chance to meet with them. The rest is up to you to make an amazing impression and show them that you are the one who can help them. But don't worry—I will lay out a process for that as well.

Jim Rohn, my all-time favorite personal-growth speaker, said, "Don't be a follower; be a student." I'm asking you to be a student as you go through the pages of this book. When you come across information that you already know or do, instead of saying, "I already do this," I encourage you to ask yourself, "How well do I do this?"

I'm grateful to join you on this journey and look forward to helping you grow in your career as a sales professional! Thank you for picking up my book. I hope it adds tremendous value to you. Happy selling!

Part 1

Before We Start Selling, Let's Prepare for the Game

CHAPTER 1
Your Success Blueprint

Know what you want and go for it as if your life
depended on it. Why? Because it does.
-Les Brown

During his seminars, Zig Ziglar would often ask the audience, "Are you a wondering generality or a meaningful specific?" He had such an amazing way with words and people. It is my belief that the difference between a person who is a meaningful specific and one who is a wondering generality is vision. As sales professionals, it is our duty to set the vision for our year, month, week, and day. Having vision gives us purpose. It gives us a reason to wake up and be enthusiastic about getting out of bed every morning. I believe that vision separates those who are extremely energetic and those who are just getting through the day. Vision allows us to create the future and know exactly what we want to achieve. When we have a picture of our desired future displayed clearly in our minds, we become enabled to focus on that goal, which then allows us to work toward that vision with all our energy. I'm inviting you to define your vision until you see it so clearly that you wake up before your alarm ever goes off to chase after it. In this chapter, I'm going to help you evoke your vision, and I cannot wait for you to experience the amazing increase in your energy levels once you have your vision established.

Have you ever woken up and had absolutely no idea what you were going to do that day? I'm not talking about your Saturday or Sunday; I'm asking about your Monday through Friday. As a young sales rep, I had days where I didn't have any appointments scheduled, and I would just drive around to find a business park to cold-call. This was in 2006, and my car was not equipped with a GPS or a smartphone! I was super cool with my flip Motorola phone and a belt clip. So that's what I did. I drove around, and when I saw a business park or an office building, I cold-called it. I was just looking for anyone in the market for a copier. Looking back at that strategy today, I can't believe how much time I wasted and how unproductive that was for my career. However, I did get comfortable with cold-calling and am very excited to share some strategies with you in the later chapters.

As a recently discharged marine, I was used to having a plan of the day in place for me. In the marines, we had everything scheduled for us—exact times to exercise, then train, then eat, then train, then eat, and then train! It's not quite like that but not too far off either. I realized it's much easier to be motivated and great at what we do when we have a plan of action in place. In the marines, we always had a plan for every day, and we executed our plan very well. I guess that's what makes marines so effective. We also thought of a few other scenarios that could potentially happen, which allowed us to be prepared so that we could react in the best way possible. If the mission completely failed, our motto was to improvise, adapt, and overcome! The point is that when I woke up in the morning, I knew what I was supposed to do to have a successful day. Just like a GPS guides me from where I am to where I need to go, this plan was my daily guide to everything I needed to achieve that day.

It was very different when I started my career in sales. There was no plan of the day, and I quickly found myself in a new place, without a clear understanding of what needed to be accomplished each day for me to be successful. I believe that many sales representatives, new and experienced, go through the same challenges.

Managers are not babysitters, and as sales professionals, we probably don't want them to be, right? Let's face it. Who can design your success better than you can? No one! That's why it's imperative that we create our own plan. If we don't, someone else will create one for us—and guess what? Their plan may not be in alignment with what we want to accomplish. In fact, most organizations have their own versions of a successful day. They use point systems to calculate your appointments, cold calls, phone calls, proposals, and so on. It's my belief that those things were beneficial before and are no longer effective in our world today. That may have been a wonderful road map in the past, but in today's world, focusing on activity does not guarantee success in sales. Focusing on helping organizations by aligning your products and services with their objectives in mind guarantees success!

What I've come to realize is that we all want to be successful, but most people don't really know what success means to them. So they go through the day reacting to everyone else's needs. They're the ones who are researching companies to call on during the day or are running around like their hair is on fire because a customer called and complained about something. I'm asking for you to not be like that. I realize that it's easier said than done, but nothing worthwhile is easy—and remember that achieving success in sales is hard work. That's why so few ever achieve it, and I know you can be one of the few. If you want to succeed in sales and you're up for the challenge, you must define what success looks like for you.

Know Where You Want to Go

Identifying your goals is one of the most important—if not *the* most important—activities you can possibly do for yourself. Why? Because having goals gives us a clear understanding of what we want to accomplish and where we want to end up. If we know where we're going, it will be much easier to get there. Think about it this way: Would you ever board an airplane without knowing its destination? I have a feeling that some of you who are reading this would. That's because you're the most adventurous risk-taking group of readers on this planet! In all seriousness, though, most people would not board that plane. I'm going to suggest that going through life without knowing where you want to end up is like boarding an airplane without knowing the destination. You'll end up somewhere, just not necessarily where you want to be.

I used to be one of those passengers, and it felt awful to go through each day without a plan, hoping things would get better but not having a clue about what better looked like. When I started planning my life and figuring out what I wanted to accomplish, everything changed. I gained a reason to wake up early, and I couldn't wait to get my day started. It was like being a little kid again (though if you ask my wife, I've always been like a little kid). I still wake up at three thirty most days. A guy needs his rest from time to time, but I don't make rest my goal.

As I began to learn more about the importance of goal setting, I came across a business teacher and a life philosopher, Jim Rohn. In addition to being known as a pioneer of personal growth, Jim authored more than seventy books and spoke all around the world on the topic of improving your life. Darren Hardy, founder of *Success magazine*, and the famous motivational speaker Tony Robbins have said that Jim Rohn was their personal mentor, and they give him credit for much of their success. During his "Best Life Ever" seminar, Jim Rohn said, "If you don't design your own life plan, chances are you'll fall into someone else's plan. And guess what they have planned for you? Not much." That statement resonated with me, and I became motivated to design my life plan—at least the first version. I must give you a fair warning that designing this plan was not easy for me to do because it took a lot of time to think quietly about what I wanted to accomplish. If you decide to take on the challenge of designing your plan, I assure you that your life will greatly improve. You will have clarity about what needs to be done because you're working toward a vision you've set for yourself. The feeling I have of knowing exactly where I'm going is truly incredible, and I know you can experience the same thing.

As simple as the task of goal setting is, many people don't actually do it. Why? I believe it's because it's easy not to set goals, and there are a few things stopping them from setting their goals:

1. *Fear of failure.* It may seem easier to not try than to try and fail. Let's face it. If we don't set goals, we'll never fail at attaining them. Right?

2. *Fear of success.* Some of us are conditioned to believe that we're not worthy of achieving success. We sabotage ourselves to not become successful on a subconscious level.

3. *Not knowing want they want.* Many people don't know what they truly want to achieve in life. They don't know their purpose. Therefore, they can't set goals to help them get there.

4. *It seems complicated.* Many of us just don't believe we have the time or capacity to sit down and think about our life and create a plan. It looks too difficult, and it's way easier to not do it.

A Better Way to Think

For many of us, when we went through the school system, we were taught what to think, not how to think. The teacher stood in the front and lectured on what happened or how something is done and then told us to read a few chapters on the subject to really learn it. If we want to establish and reach goals, we can't think with the same thought process that got us to where we are today. We must use the creative, imaginative side of our brains. If we use the same thought process that got us to this point—and believe me, everything we have accomplished to this date is a direct result of our very best thinking—there is no way for us to ever achieve more. To achieve what we haven't yet achieved, we must think what we haven't yet thought!

Conclusion

Many people take more time to plan their weekend than they take to plan their life. Those are the same people who are working in jobs they don't want to work in, living where they don't want to live, driving what they don't want to drive, and just letting life happen to them instead of being in control of their life. I'm asking you to design the life you want for yourself. It will give you a sense of accomplishment and complete clarity on what you need to do next to get you closer to the life you've designed for yourself.

This book is designed to help you improve your sales skills. Each chapter will teach a lesson on something crucial to help you become a successful sales professional. At the end of each chapter, there will be a review of the chapter along with an exercise to help you begin mastering the topic of the chapter. If you've read other sales books and skipped over the exercises, I encourage you to do it differently this time. It's important not only to read but also to do, so that you retain information better. If you're serious about improving as a sales professional, these exercises will prove to be extremely beneficial as you read the chapters ahead.

I look forward to seeing you in the next chapter ... after you complete the following exercise!

Clarify Your Vision, Purpose, and Goals

If I had the opportunity to coach you one-on-one, the first thing we would do is set your destination and define what it is you would like to achieve. By taking your time to complete this exercise, you will take the first and toughest step toward committing to excellence. You will experience a greater satisfaction in everything you do toward achieving your goals, and you will be excited to wake up each day so you can chase the things you know you want to achieve.

Please take the time you need to answer the following questions. You will gain the best results by thinking through each question and being completely honest with yourself. Good luck!

- What do I want? (Write out all the things that come to mind. Let your imagination go crazy!)

- Who is my ideal client? (Company size? Revenue? Location? Industry?)

- How can I help them?

- How much money do I want to make?
  - » Per year?
  - » Per month?
  - » Per sale?

- What type of person do I want to become?
  - » Personally?
  - » Professionally?
  - » With my family?
  - » With my friends?
  - » With my colleagues?

- Wouldn't it be great if …
    - » I donated $_____ to (organization of choice) by month/day/year
    - » I experienced _____
    - » I owned _____
    - » I traveled to_____
    - » I learned how to_____

- If I had a magic wand, what would I create?

- What's stopping me from creating it?

CHAPTER 2
The Secret Way to Start Your Day

The best part of waking up is not
Folgers in your cup!

Now that you have a clear vision of what you're trying to achieve, it's important to develop the right habits to make each day as successful as possible. How we show up to see our clients is extremely important, especially in a sales role. In our B2B world, people don't buy from companies, they buy from people. That's why so many sales reps can take their clients with them wherever they go, and companies are forced to create noncompete documents for reps to abide by. So, how do you show up? Not just physically but mentally, spiritually, and emotionally as well. Are you 100 percent engaged, listening with curiosity, and focused on your client's needs? Or are you zoning out, thinking about what you're going to have for dinner, or how you may be losing an account, or how your significant other is the best person ever? Is your mind focused, or is it all over the place? The last question I'll ask is this: Are your customers getting the best you possible?

Unfortunately, I had to learn this the hard way. It took about eighteen months for me to go from being in very good shape when I departed from the marines to the worst shape of my life. In that time frame, I gained over fifty pounds and stopped exercising. So, with the loss of muscle and a tremendous increase in fat, I probably looked like I had gained over a hundred pounds. The worst thing was that I didn't even know it. The way I found out was when my wife, Julia, joined me on one of the first President's Club trips that I won for having exceeded my sales quota. The trip was at a beautiful all-inclusive resort in Mexico where we had tons of fun at the beach, were treated like royalty the whole time we were there, and got to experience what it feels like to win in sales. If your company has incentives to win trips, make sure you're one of the winners. If you're not, then you're the one who's paying for the winners to go on the trip! After we returned home, Julia asked me to look through the pictures from our trip and pulled up a specific one for me to look at. When she asked what I thought of this picture, in which she looked amazing, I couldn't understand who the chubby guy in the picture was. Okay, I'm being nice; the guy was way past chubby. As you've probably already guessed, I was looking at myself and did not recognize me. It was a huge blow to my ego to see what I had turned myself into in such a short time. I quickly decided to make some changes in my life. I began by changing what I was eating and starting a workout routine.

Since evenings were taken up with working and spending time with Julia, I decided to start working out early in the morning, at five o'clock. It took around two months for my routine to become a habit, and I'm proud to say that I'm still following it … most of the time! When I started to wake up earlier to exercise, my energy levels increased, my self-confidence improved, and I felt so much better! The biggest takeaway here is not the working out; it's the fact that I started taking care of myself, which allowed my coworkers and customers to get the best of me, like they deserved.

My morning routine has evolved since those days. Today, I have six things that I like to make a part of my every morning; however, four of them are always a must. I'll share all six with you, and I highly recommend creating a morning routine for yourself that will help you take on the day. It's important to understand that while this routine works for me, it may not be the exact one that works for you. If you find that my routine is not something that could help you, I encourage you to create one that would fit your life better. The important takeaway in this section is to intentionally design a morning that will help bring you closer to your vision—on a daily basis.

When I became certified as a coach through the John Maxwell Team, I decided to hire my own coach to see what that process is like from the side of the person who's being coached. I hired Julie Reisler (http://juliereisler.com/), a highly recommended coach and author of Get a PhD in YOU, which is a step-by-step guide to designing your life. Julie is wonderful. As my coach, she helped me uncover areas of my life where I was stuck. Please keep in mind that most people would never know that I was stuck in anything by looking at me. As a matter of fact, I had no idea that I was stuck either. My income exceeded six figures, I was doing great at work, my family life was good, and there weren't many things that I wanted that I wasn't able to get. I'm not saying this to boast; I'm saying this to share that even if we're doing great in our lives, we can still be stuck. I was stuck in the area of growing my sales team at DCA Imaging Systems and at my company, the Goal Guide. The main reason was that I didn't have a clear understanding of what I wanted to accomplish, and to be completely honest, I didn't have a vision for my life. This all changed once I started to work with Julie. She helped me think through various areas of my life that I thought could use improvement.

The best thing Julie and I did together was design my perfect morning, which changed my life. I noticed that I had a plan of action each day. As a matter of fact, I knew what my whole week was going to look like on Sunday evening. It was exciting to wake up each day with a few goals that I wanted to accomplish, each one taking me closer to growing my sales team at DCA and attracting more clients at the Goal Guide. Eventually, my morning routine led me to writing this book, something I never thought I would do. As I share my routine with you, I encourage you to think of ways you can implement some of the things that have helped me. Once an idea comes to you, the best thing you can do is schedule it on your calendar so that you can be more committed to taking action on your wonderful idea.

The six activities I strive to complete every morning are as follows:

1. Write/Journal
2. Reflect
3. Meditate
4. Think
5. Pray
6. Exercise

The reason this morning routine has been so helpful for me is because it allows me to take care of myself first. It prepares me for each day, physically, mentally, and spiritually, which ensures that I show up completely prepared for any task, with the highest confidence and the best attitude. This is a great combination for a professional salesperson.

Write/Journal

The first thing Julie worked with me on was journaling. I could not understand how journaling had anything to do with being successful. It almost felt like I had to keep a diary. Okay, it felt exactly like that. But I knew that if I wanted different results in my life, I needed to start doing different things. So, I gave it a shot—and boy did it work. It's still hard for me to explain the benefits of writing first thing in the morning. As a matter of fact, when I began doing it, I rarely had a clue of what I was supposed to be writing, but Julie said, "Just write your thoughts." I don't know about you, but when I get up first thing in the morning, it feels like there are hundreds of thoughts running through my mind. What meetings do I have? What am I working on today? Who do I need to call? What do the kids have going on? Someone said something yesterday … what did they mean by that? The list of thoughts and questions could take up a few pages in this book! The main thing journaling has allowed me to do is to separate myself from these thoughts. By writing them down, I am no longer thinking them. I can see these questions, thoughts, and problems on a piece of paper, which gives me an opportunity to evaluate them and solve them, if necessary. There is something magical about getting our thoughts on paper. For example, if we write down our thoughts and ideas, we won't forget them. Have you ever had an amazing idea and later you couldn't remember what it was? Journaling allows us to capture those ideas and to potentially act on them at a later time. I'll talk more about that when I describe reflection.

So, what can you write about? Well, to make it easy, you can start by writing out how you're feeling today and what you're thinking about. Then you can write all the things you'd like to accomplish today. Be specific and detailed. And have fun with it! You can even write down to call a person you haven't seen in a while, or challenge yourself to commit to a certain number of prospecting calls. There is no wrong way to journal, so go for it and see how it impacts your life. Worst-case scenario is that you'll try and it won't do anything for you, which means you'll end up exactly where you are today. But what if it does work wonders for your life and career? I recommend you give it a shot for one month and see what happens.

As a coach, I recommend journaling to all my clients. The ones who decide to try it experience tremendous results. They absolutely love clearing their minds first thing in the morning, and I'm certain you will experience similar results.

Reflect

I call reflecting a hidden secret for growth. The way I do it is by thinking about the day before or the entire week up until the point of reflection. I recall the conversations I had with people in all aspects of my life. I try to remember how I felt before, during, and after those conversations. I then think of things I could have done differently. I place myself in others' shoes and try to think of how they perceived our conversation or situation at hand. I then think of things that I could have done better than I did and make a mental note of how to handle similar situations in the future.

The importance of reflecting is to learn from our past and to avoid making the same mistakes moving forward. When I started in copier sales and had a tough time scheduling appointments and closing sales, I was told, "Sales is a numbers game." Have you heard this silliness? Just keep dialing, and eventually you'll schedule an appointment. There are managers today who have the same mentality. Unfortunately, it took me way too long to realize this, but sales is not a numbers game. Just because you make more calls doesn't mean you'll be successful at scheduling an appointment with your prospective client. I realize that even a blind squirrel will find an acorn one day, but it's much more effective to pause, reflect on your progress, and make the necessary adjustments to improve your results, isn't it? If you follow any NFL team, you see the quarterback looking at pictures of previous plays on the sidelines after throwing an interception. Why do they do this? Because it gives them an opportunity to see what they missed the first time and to avoid the same mistake in the future. Also, there is nothing more frustrating than seeing your favorite team get completely beat on defense during the first half of the game, only to go into the second half without making any adjustments. Have you been there before? I have, and it's not a good feeling. We tend to expect our favorite sports professionals to see what happened, adjust, and do better. By reflecting, we're giving ourselves the same opportunity.

To improve our chances of success when making phone calls to new prospective clients, reflection will allow us to analyze what we're saying and how we sound. It will also give us an opportunity to think about whether or not we would agree to a meeting with ourselves if we were the person receiving the call. It's tough to see the picture from inside the frame, and we all have the tendency to think we're doing great. Reflection allows us to step out of the frame and see the picture as a whole. It's only when we see that picture clearly that we're able to make the necessary adjustments to achieve better results. Just like the quarterback on the sidelines.

Meditate

Meditation helps us train our minds to relax and stay focused throughout the day. In the wonderful profession of sales, many surprises pop up each day, not to mention the emotional stress our minds endure daily. Anyone who's successful in sales is passionate about helping their clients, creating solutions, and winning. We put our hearts into every opportunity, stay up late thinking about solutions and writing proposals, and try to build relationships with every step of the sales cycle. The harsh reality is that it doesn't guarantee a win. We can do everything correctly, have an amazing rapport, provide the best solution, and still, the client might make a decision solely on price or might be overruled by someone higher in their organization to keep what they have.

I wish I had a magical process to close every deal or to schedule an appointment with a prospect every time we make a call. Unfortunately, that doesn't exist. However, what I can teach you is to be more effective to increase your chances every time. This is where meditation can really help. Think of it this way. In a span of a few hours, a sales professional can win a huge deal, lose a huge deal, get rejected multiple times, and schedule a few meetings. Not to mention all the calls we might receive from customers with complaints or emergencies that need our immediate attention. Being in sales is an emotional roller coaster, if we allow it to be.

Meditation allows me to control my thoughts and keep my mind sharp and calm during emotional peaks and valleys, as much as possible, throughout the day. The first time someone recommended that I meditate, I had no clue of what to do! They said, "Just close your eyes and watch your thoughts." And I thought, What the hell does that mean? So, I did what every normal person would do—nothing! Until months later when a good friend of mine introduced me to an app called Headspace. The download is free, and the first ten days are also free. Headspace provided a guided meditation for ten minutes per day, which, for someone like me, was perfect. Everyone knows that you can't keep a salesperson's attention for more than ten minutes; our minds are usually off and away, figuring out how to sell something. I decided to purchase a full year of guided meditation through this app and have been impressed with the outcome since. It allows me to stay calm during the times when I used to want to scream at the top of my lungs. Perhaps it could do the same for you. By the way, I'm not in any way, shape, or form affiliated with this app. Those guys have no idea I'm recommending them. I just want to share my tools with you so that you have more options available to you as you embark on your journey of improvement.

Think

Now that our minds are clear because we journaled, we reflected on previous experiences, and we focused our minds through meditation, I recommend that we think. You may be saying, "I already think all the time." What I'm talking about is a specific type of thinking. This is where you pick something that's on your mind and intentionally think through accomplishing that task. When I first started writing this book, I had no idea where to start, how to start, what to say first, and how it was going to be laid out. All of those unknowns kept me in a hesitation to begin. One day I decided to think through the how of getting this book published, and I began with an outline. It took dedicated time, with a specific topic to think about, to really make progress—and the rest is history.

Thinking allows us to take the information we found through journaling, reflection, and meditation and channel it in a way that helps us use it to our benefit. Thinking allows us to look at the things we want to accomplish and create a detailed plan to make it happen. Thinking helps us generate ideas that will help us stand out in competitive situations. Napoleon Hill wrote one of the most popular books of all time, called Think and Grow Rich, after studying the lives of the most successful people for twenty years. Isn't that something? Think and Grow Rich—what a title! What if it's true—and we still don't take time to intentionally think? That would be a shame, wouldn't it? Every wonderful thing that has ever been created or achieved started with a thought. Knowing this, we can now become intentional about taking time out of our day to think.

If you can commit to ten minutes of intentional thinking about a specific area in your life, perhaps an area of improvement, in the morning, I assure you that you will generate amazing ideas to help you increase your influence and sell more to your potential clients.

Pray

I know that speaking about God is not something we typically do in sales books, so feel free to skip this section if you feel more comfortable that way. I won't get upset, I promise! I feel like being authentic with you is the best way for me to be, and if I were to leave this section out, I wouldn't be authentic. If there is something that helps me be successful in my career, I want to share it with you in case it helps you too.

I'm a novice when it comes to my spiritual journey, so there is not much that I can offer from personal experience as it pertains to praying. However, I try to do it in the morning before leaving the house, and the feeling I get as soon as I'm done is incredible. I feel like I become connected to my higher power, like I'm in a relationship, where God is looking out for me. I make sure to express gratitude for everything I have in my life. I ask for strength to help me make the right decisions during the toughest times. And I ask for God to look after my family, friends, and people who come to mind at that time. If prayer is a part of your daily routine, then you probably know what I'm talking about. If not, perhaps it could help you feel a stronger connection. The reason I wanted to share this with you is because when we feel that connection, we're more confident in our abilities to do the "scary" things. We're better equipped to take on any challenge, and there seems to be a feeling of God having our back, no matter what kind of risk we take.

Exercise

If our minds aren't clear and ready to take on the day by this point, I don't know if there's anything we could do to help them get there! The last thing I do for my morning routine is exercise. I don't know all the scientific benefits of exercising, but I can tell you from personal experience that it sets the right tone for my day. If there's an ounce of stress left after I journal, reflect, meditate, think, and pray, exercising eliminates it for me! It allows me to stay in good shape and greatly improves my confidence.

Earlier, I asked, "How are you showing up?" Even though we say that people aren't supposed to judge us by the way we look, they do. So why not show up in the best possible physical condition we can create for ourselves? What I know is that people want to be around confident people. They want to be with people who make them feel good about themselves, and before we can make anyone else feel good, we should feel good about ourselves. This is where working out comes into play.

Conclusion

My morning routine has worked for me and for many of the people I have had the honor of coaching. The six morning activities shared in this chapter have tremendously improved my life emotionally, physically, financially, and professionally. I'm excited to have had the opportunity to share them with you, and I hope you will have similar results.

If you are interested in making changes to your morning routine, I recommend you take it one step at a time, or it can become frustrating and overwhelming. Remember—this is a marathon, not a sprint. Start with journaling and see what that does for you. Then you can either keep it and add something else, like reflection, or skip it and just try to exercise before starting your day. Whatever you decide to implement that you're currently not doing will be a great step for improvement—personally, emotionally, and professionally.

Remember when we board a plane, before takeoff, the flight attendant gives the usual demonstration. During this demonstration, they show the passengers how to use the oxygen mask if it ever falls out from the above compartment. They always say to place the mask on yourself first before helping others around you. Having a morning routine, like the one I shared with you, is me asking you to place the oxygen mask on yourself first. When you're the best you can be, you'll be able to provide your clients and potential clients with the attention and service levels they truly deserve. You'll be able to really stand out from the rest!

Create Your Morning Routine

When I began implementing a morning routine, my life changed for the better. There was something special about having a plan of action as soon as I woke up every morning, and it gave me a sense of accomplishment early in the day. Having a routine sets us up for success. It's a starting point to designing the life we want to live instead of just going through the motions, and it helps make setting and reaching our goals easier.

To make sure you set yourself up for success, I recommend that you start by making a small change instead of changing everything at once. We can break this down by weeks or even months, if that's more comfortable for you. The key is to do something small right away and feel great about your results.

Week (or Month) 1: Wake up fifteen minutes earlier to write in your journal.
- Write down everything that comes to mind. Just run free with it.

Week (or Month) 2: Wake up another fifteen minutes earlier to reflect after you journal.
- Think about yesterday and answer the following three questions:
  1. What went right?
  2. What went wrong?
  3. What can I do to improve what happened?

Week (or Month) 3: Wake up another fifteen minutes earlier to meditate.
- Find a quiet place.
- Get some headphones and meditate. (Earlier, I recommended the Headspace app if you've never meditated before. I recently found out that YouTube has free ten- to fifteen-minute guided meditation sessions as well. I've been using them to meditate, and it's been wonderful. Try one for a week and then try the other the following week; see which one you like better.)

Week (or Month) 4: Wake up another fifteen minutes earlier to think.

- Create a place in your house where you can think.
- Ask yourself the following questions:
  1. What do I want to accomplish today?
  2. Who do I want to schedule a meeting with today?
  3. What do I want to learn today?
  4. In what area would I like to improve today?

Week (or Month) 5: Wake up another five minutes earlier to pray and give thanks.

- If spirituality is not your cup of tea and you don't feel comfortable praying, that's okay. It's not for everyone. In this case, think of a few things in your life that you're thankful for. This will help you start your day focusing on the positive things in your life, which will lead to a more positive you everywhere you go!

Week (or Month) 6: Wake up another fifteen minutes earlier to exercise.

- If you exercise in the evening, that's wonderful. Still do something first thing in the morning to get the blood flowing.
- Complete three sets of push-ups, sit-ups, squats, and jumping jacks.
- Go at your own pace.

The plan above reflects how I would do it if I were starting over again. The important takeaway is that you start small and go at your own pace. Once you see improvement in your life, you will be encouraged to go faster and bigger! When I first started, I was waking up at six thirty. Today, my alarm is set for three thirty, and on some days, I wake up at a quarter after three.

The amount of extra time that I gained by waking up early allowed me to get into the best shape of my life, earn the most amount of money I've ever earned, read more books that I ever read, generate amazing ideas that helped my sales team grow their revenues and incomes, and write this book. The best part is that I gain an extra eighty-four hours per month (3 hours saved x 7 days per week = 21 hours x 4 weeks per month = 84 hours) to do what I need to do in order to create the life I want. Many people use "not having time" as an excuse. The steps outlined in this chapter guarantee that time will no longer be an issue.

I'm positive that implementing a morning routine can do great things in your life, and I wish you the best of luck!

CHAPTER 3
TGIS Mindset of the Top 1%

If you fail to plan, you're planning to fail.
-Benjamin Franklin

The final step in preparing is planning our week for success. I couldn't be more excited about this topic! Having a plan for the week helps us maximize our time and focus on selling during the peak selling times, instead of figuring out who to call and where to sell. It allows us to mentally design the week and see what we're going to do, who we're going to call, and who we will meet with. It helps us plan out what we're going to say in the important situations that may yield to generating income.

The act of *planning the week* is similar to the act of *thinking* that I mentioned as part of my morning routine. As a matter of fact, it takes a lot of thinking to plan a great week. The difference here is that you're going to plan your week only once each week, whereas intentional thinking should occur every morning. Also, the intentional thinking during your morning routine will usually focus on a specific account you're working on, how to create extra wealth, improving your family's lifestyle … pretty much anything that's on your mind. When planning for the week, it requires thinking only about the week ahead.

Before GPS systems were affordable, we used to type the address of where we were going into mapquest.com and print out the directions before leaving the office. Today, just about everyone in sales has a GPS in their car or on their phone to help guide them to their location. I even use the Waze app to get home from the office every day because it reroutes me in case there is an accident and lets me know if there are police officers on my route so I can slow down. I absolutely love having a GPS system to guide me!

When we get in our cars to drive somewhere, we know exactly where we're going and what we're trying to accomplish (most of the time). There are occasions when you just want to drive a scenic route without having much more of a purpose than enjoying the drive. However, you still have a purpose and an understanding of what you're trying to accomplish in that case. Unfortunately, many people don't apply that mind-set to their week. They simply don't know what they would like to accomplish by the end of each week; therefore, just let the week happen to them. When I ask salespeople how they know if their week was successful, I often receive answers like "If I made a sale, it was successful." When I dig deeper and ask, "How much does the sale have to be?" they seldom have an answer, and on a few occasions, I hear someone say, "Any sale is a good week."

I'm asking you to be better than that. Successful people in any career, but especially in sales, have a solid plan and know exactly where they want to end up each week. They take the time to plan each week and schedule activities that will ensure they generate the income they desire. The best part is they never wake up wondering what to do that day. The destination of their GPS has been set for the week, and now they're just following it along to the path of success that they identified for themselves.

By now you might be thinking, *Why did I buy this book? I wanted to learn about improving my sales skills, and this goofy guy is writing about mind-set, goal setting, productive mornings, and planning a week.* You're right—almost! If you've ever watched the original *Karate Kid*, you'll remember how Daniel was frustrated with Mr. Miyagi when he wanted to learn how to fight, and his teacher had him painting a fence and waxing the car. What was Mr. Miyagi doing? He was preparing Daniel physically and mentally for the challenges he would have to overcome. That's exactly what I'm doing here. If you've ever attended or watched a business success or personal development seminar, instructors like John Maxwell, Brian Tracy, Tony Robbins, and Jim Rohn all teach that if we prepare a plan for each week and have our minds focused on all the right things, we'll be able to "crane kick" the crap out of our competition and win more often than we lose (not in those exact words!). After hearing the message about the need to have a specific plan echoed by so many successful people, I decided to put it to the test myself, and it drastically improved the way I conduct business. My sales increased, and my time is used more efficiently to maximize my results.

Many of us just don't have a clear understanding of how to plan and what to plan. As soon as we begin our planning process, our minds automatically convince us to not schedule so many things in case someone needs our attention. I also realize that it's easier to not prepare for the week, it's easier to not wake up in the morning and work on yourself, and it's easier to not be a rock star in sales. But I don't believe that's what you want for your life. I think you're motivated and ready to take the steps you need to take to be on the next President's Club trip, or in the top performers' club, or to grow your business and be financially independent. You are a star already. Now let's help you shine brighter!

Think Like a Business Owner

Unless you're on a commission only type of compensation plan, it's easy to continue viewing your sales career as a job instead of your own business. However, if you want to be successful in sales, it helps to view yourself as a business owner instead of a person with a nine-to-five job. I assure you that having this type of philosophy will help set you up for success and will be very beneficial in assisting you to grow your business as a passionate business owner. In his book *Think and Grow Rich*, Napoleon Hill tells a story about an ancient group of warriors who took their naval fleet to capture an island where they were outnumbered, with very little chance of winning the battle. The commander of that group ordered the men to burn their ships before going into battle. Once the ships were in flames, he told the men that the only way they were going home was if they won. The story goes that they won. Napoleon uses this example to illustrate that when we have nothing to fall back on and we must do something to survive, we have a greater chance of success. If we "burn our ships" mentally and start believing that if we don't succeed, we'll perish, we have no other choice but to become successful "business owners" in our position as sales professionals.

In my last year in the marines, after eight years of service, I was making around $27,000 per year in salary, plus a few hundred bucks per month for housing and food. I'm not complaining, just putting things in perspective and sharing a mind-changing moment in my career. I realize that I didn't mention all the amazing benefits I was receiving for health care, but that's because I really didn't understand the financial value of it back then. When I accepted my first job as a sales representative, it was based on a draw, and I was being paid $40,000 per year, which was awesome for me, considering what I was making in my previous role. At that time, it was easy for me to get comfortable and just sell the minimum to make my guaranteed base pay. Let's face it. Even if I didn't sell anything, I would make more money than I was making before. I'm not too sure how long I would have been able to keep that position, though—not to mention it would have been the wrong attitude. I made a few sales early but nothing too crazy. It wasn't until my sixth month that I closed a good amount of business and received a commission check of $7,500 on top of my regular pay. I couldn't believe my eyes. I was an immigrant kid who grew up poor and slept in one bedroom with three sisters. I did not have a college degree at that time, and I was able to earn around $10,000 in one month! That, my friend, was a huge eye-opener for me. That's when I realized that there were no limits on my earning potential in the world of sales, and I could control my destiny by working harder and smarter, if I chose to do so. That was when I told myself that I never wanted to make a commission check less than $7,500. It was the goal I strove toward every month, and my second full year with the company, I attained that goal and made the President's Club trip!

Looking at your job as your own business produces better results for you. It places you under healthy pressure to perform, and it greatly improves your attitude at work, which could turn into a promotion to leading other salespeople. It makes you more valuable to your company and your customers, and it helps turn you into a person who others want to conduct business with. One of the things tenured salespeople say in a competitive situation is "I do this to support my family, not for beer money." I'm asking you to not be the person who's perceived as someone who's in this position for the beer money. People will not take you seriously—trust me!

Being Busy Does Not Equal Productivity

One valuable lesson I learned is that sales winners understand that between the hours of 9:00 a.m. and 5:00 p.m., in most industries, they can maximize their selling time by focusing on being in front of potential clients. So, I followed their lead. However, we all know that there are way too many other things that sales professionals are tasked with daily. They must prospect for new business, create proposals, write thank-you notes, fill out paperwork, put out fires, pop in to see potential clients, and continually learn about their products, services, and industry. That's a hefty list, isn't it?

As you can see, it's very easy to become distracted and busy in the world of sales while losing productive time in front of prospective clients. Unfortunately, many sales professionals fall into this never-ending busywork, which prevents them from being client facing and sets them up for failure. Sometimes, it's completely justified, and emergency situations occur. But most of the time, salespeople fall into the whirlwind of busywork because they don't have a clear plan of what they should be doing, so they believe that doing anything is good.

Remember busy does not equal productive. Jim Rohn said, "Most people major in minor things." I'm asking you to not do that! Let's find the key things that will help you increase your sales revenues and focus on them so that you're not one of the people majoring in minor things. Let's set your weekly destinations on your GPS and watch how your income increases as a result of you becoming a person with a plan.

Thank God It's Sunday (TGIS)—Best Time to Plan the Week

Since I didn't want to take up valuable selling time planning my week, I decided to do all my planning every Sunday evening. Now, you may be thinking that your company doesn't pay you on Sunday evening, and I'm once again asking you to change that thought process and think like a business owner. Remember—if you want to succeed in this career, it will serve you better to view your territory as your own company that you're trying to grow. It needs you thinking about it 24-7! Okay, maybe not that dramatic, but at least an hour or two on Sunday evening to get you started in the right direction for the upcoming week. I know that since you're reading this book, you're a great student and you're willing to give this a try. Please take a few seconds right now to block off time in your calendar for planning your week ahead.

When the time comes to plan the week, you're going to first set your GPS by asking yourself the following questions:

- What do I want to accomplish this week? (Write it out and clearly see your plan.)
- How many appointments will I commit to scheduling?
- What times will I block off to do so? (Block the times on your calendar.)
- How many calls will I commit to making? (Block the times on your calendar.)
- What networking events would I like to attend?

Once you've answered these questions, you've set your GPS. Congratulations!

The next step is research, and it requires discipline. Do you have what it takes to stay focused on your objective of increasing your sales and income? Will you be able to stay committed to your commitments? Research is crucial to a salesperson's success, but many people skip it because it's way easier to not do it.

Research

You can quickly rise to the top percentile of your organization if you take the time to research the companies and people that you'd like to reach out to prior to entering the week. It will be a tremendous time-saver during selling hours if you can research who you're going after during your Sunday-evening planning. This will give you an incredible jump over your competition. Think about how many of your coworkers sit in the office during the day to research who they want to call. I believe that some of that is due to procrastination and call reluctance, but we can save that for the next book. Researching during nonselling hours will allow you to sell more while your competitors are researching. It's a tremendous advantage if you can discipline yourself to do it.

Instead of being hypothetical, let's try this together because, even though it sounds simple, many salespeople have a tough time focusing on the task at hand. It's way too easy to get lost in the never-ending world of the internet once we start researching anything. Yes, or yes? I remember starting to research an energy drink distributor, and I ended up watching a bunch of X-games videos on YouTube because those were some of the links connected to the searches I was Googling. The worst part was that I spent over an hour watching videos and still knew nothing about the company I was trying to research! I can laugh about it now, but I want to help you avoid those mistakes by guiding you through this process and giving you the questions to ask yourself when researching a company.

The goal of researching is to have a clear understanding of what the organization is about and who would be interested in your products or services. Sounds simple, right? Here are some things that would be beneficial for you to understand prior to making your initial contact to schedule an introduction meeting. Feel free to create one of these for each of the companies you research and have it in front of you (maybe scan it into your CRM system too) when making your calls.

Name of the company:
Company's mission (website, Google, LinkedIn):
Company's products are:
Company's services are:
Company's target market is:
Company's competitors are:
Name of first desired contact:

Title:

Phone number:

Previous experience:

College:

Interests:

Why would this person benefit from my product or service?

You can go into much more detail with your research, but for now, I want to keep it as simple as possible. It's important that you start doing this ASAP and get as much information as you can. Even a little bit of info can place you heads and shoulders above your competition, because your calls are going to be more purposeful and directed toward helping the company improve something or increase revenues. I ask that, as you create this habit in your life, you seek to modify and improve your search criteria to best fit the business model that works for you. If you're selling directly to consumers, your search may be limited to social media platforms like LinkedIn, Facebook, Twitter, Instagram, and any other new one that may have popped up by now. The main value that I hope you take away from this exercise is to never call someone unless you know something about them and their organization.

Unfortunately for me, I had to learn this lesson the hard way. When I first started out in sales, my success was measured by my activity levels (or at least it seemed that way.) Since my manager was constantly pressured to get the team's number of calls up, that became the main topic of our meetings. And because I didn't want to go into his office without having at least a hundred calls made in the previous week, I tended to concentrate more on the quantity of the calls I was making instead of the quality. Needless to say, I did not research much. The most embarrassing moment came when I blindly dialed a company to speak with the person who was listed as the contact in my CRM, and the woman who picked up told me he passed away. To make matters worse, that person died over a year prior to me calling, and the woman I spoke with was his wife. I could have avoided the embarrassment if I had just taken some time to understand whom I was calling on and why.

Another reason it's important to research and have a list of people ready to call is because momentum plays a huge role when making calls. The last thing you want to do is research a company between every call you make. If you schedule an appointment and feel like you're in the zone, it's important to continue to make calls without interruptions. There is nothing better than making three calls and scheduling three appointments in a row. Do not break the momentum by researching the company right before calling; instead, have your completed research notes in front of you as you're making calls.

Final Thought

As I mentioned before, sales is not easy, and not everyone is cut out for it. But if you've made your decision to be a sales professional, I'm asking you to adopt the disciplines that will make you successful. I love how the late Jim Rohn defined success. In his book *The Five Major Pieces to the Life Puzzle*, Mr. Rohn said, "Success is a few simple disciplines practiced every day." And it's so true, isn't it? If we exercise and eat right, there is a good chance that we will be successful at maintaining a healthy weight. If we meditate daily, we'll most likely see success in staying calm during stressful situations and being more focused. If we spend an hour per day to learn something new about a topic we're interested in, we will be considered an expert in that field within five years. The best thing we can do right now, no matter where we are in our career, is to identify and develop the daily disciplines that will help us be successful. Let me repeat that because it's such an important point! *The best thing we can do right now, no matter where we are in our career, is to identify and develop the daily disciplines that will help us be successful.* I'm going to suggest that by having a clear vision and purpose for what you want to accomplish, creating a morning routine that focuses on getting your mind and body into an optimum state, and researching the people you want to turn into customers, prior to calling on them, you will be leaps and bounds above other professionals in your field. Ultimately, you will be able to bring greater value to your clients, which they will see from a mile away!

Create Your Weekly Plan

The most important takeaway from this chapter is setting your GPS on Sunday evening. There is something special about taking the time to plan the week ahead. What I've noticed is that when I began planning my weeks, I was more excited to wake up and get to work on Monday morning. I was a man with a purpose, on a mission to make something special happen. You can be a person with a purpose, on your mission to make something special happen as well.

To help you set your GPS, please answer the following questions:

- What appointments do I have scheduled this week?
  - » What research needs to be done for each one?
    - * Name of the company:
    - * Company's mission (website, Google, LinkedIn):
    - * Company's products are:
    - * Company's services are:
    - * Company's target market is:
    - * Company's competitors are:
    - * Name of first desired contact:
      - Title:
      - Phone number:
      - Previous experience:
      - College:
      - Interests:
      - Why would this person benefit from my product or service?

- What do I want to accomplish this week? (Write it out and clearly see your plan.)

- How many appointments will I commit to scheduling?

- What times will I block off to do so? (Block the times on your calendar.)

- How many calls will I commit to making? (Block the times on your calendar.)

- What networking events would I like to attend?

If you've answered the questions above, it's a good idea to plug your plan into your calendar. This way, you have everything scheduled, just as you would an important meeting. The key is to treat your planned activities as a meeting. Just as you wouldn't cancel one appointment for something else, do not cancel your appointed scheduling time for something else either. Commit to your commitments, and no matter what, follow through with your plan to arrive at your set destination.

Part 2

Let's Go on an Amazing Adventure Called the Buyer's Journey

CHAPTER 4
The 10 Steps to Closing the Deal

A leader is one who knows the way, goes the way,
and shows the way.
–John C. Maxwell

If I were to ask you to show me your sales process, what would you show me? Are you one of the people who says, "Whatever my client says, that's my process"? Or would you actually be able to give me a detailed explanation of your sales process? I like to call my sales process a buyer's journey. It sounds so much nicer, and I think people love being on a journey way more than they like being in a sales process! I want to caution you that if I ever deviate from the buyer's journey, it will be in extremely rare cases. There are occasions where the customers know exactly what they want, they've done all their research, and all they need to do now is purchase whatever they've decided on. Even in those cases, I would still inquire about how they chose the product as the one for them. If their answer is good and they've truly done their research, I'd sell it to them without presenting another option. There aren't many more types of scenarios where I would deviate from my process.

I designed my buyer's journey after reflecting on my many failures and losses of opportunities. I want to make sure that you're well equipped to avoid my mistakes. It took me a while to sit down after each loss and see what I did wrong. This is also a great discipline to implement when we win deals. Reflecting to see why we won or lost greatly helps us to not make the same mistake or to repeat what works. I'm glad to say that the buyer's journey, which I'll share with you, is a compilation of strategies that worked for me.

Another reason the buyer's journey is extremely important is because it allows for many checks and balances. It ensures that our client will ultimately receive the best product or service to help them improve their specific situation. It provides us with a platform to not only build rapport with our clients but also build a relationship to continue partnering with them after the initial sale. As a sales manager, there have been more times than I can remember when I would visit a client after their sales rep left our organization. It might be a check-in, or sometimes they had a proposal on the table for an upgrade or additional services. What bothered me most, and still does, is when I heard our client say that the sales rep really didn't do that much, or that they didn't have a relationship with that person. I've heard things like "The only time we'd see our rep was when he was trying to sell us something." On several occasions, customers told me that they never saw the rep again after the sale. I can attest that in the office equipment world, every company says that they're going to conduct quarterly reviews with all of their clients, but few actually do it, and that's unfortunate. What do you promise to your clients before the sale is made? Do you always keep your promise? If not, why not?

Before you start thinking that I'm bashing sales reps and acting like I've never made a mistake, let me assure you that I'm as guilty of this as everyone else, and probably even worse. The only reason I'm able to shed light on it now is because I've had the pleasure of hearing what the customers thought after finding out their rep left. Every time I heard something negative about a former sales rep, I could always remember a time where I made the same mistake, without realizing it. If you're reading this as a sales representative, please take into consideration the fact that even if you leave the company you're currently with, you'll be able to continue the relationship with your client regardless of the products you sell … if you treat them like a friend.

It's unfortunate that many people go for the sale instead of a relationship these days. I'm asking you to go for the relationship instead of the sale! If you do a good job building the relationship, I guarantee that the sale will happen. It may not be with this person; however, if you maintain the rapport, even if you lose the sale, they will refer you to their friends and will possibly use you for future business. Remember what our friend Zig said, "You can have everything in life that you want if you help enough other people achieve what they want."

If we take our time and define the journey that we want our client to experience, it will be easier for us to build rapport and create friendships that last as long as we want them to. They will be friendships based on trust, loyalty, integrity, and truly having the other person's best interests in mind. Very few salespeople have these types of relationships; however, the ones who do reap the rewards every single day. They're the ones whose clients we call on and hear, "I'll never switch from my vendor." How many of your clients will say that about you if we were to call them right now? If you can't think of many, perhaps it's time to change your approach. What do you think?

My goal is to provide you with the tools that you can pick up and use to help you grow your business. By applying the following principles, you will be better equipped to initiate a conversation with potential clients, create long-lasting relationships, and take care of your clients in such a way that they tell all their friends about your amazing service! Here is the buyer's journey that I've been speaking about:

- initial contact (cold-calling, phone calls, emails, strategic stop by, networking)
- introduction meeting
- analysis
- proof of concept / demonstration
- validation meeting
- proposal
- close
- implementation meeting
- postsale
- becoming a magnet for referrals

These are the steps I try to check off in every sales process, and I will go into greater detail about each one in the chapters that follow. I'll also go into detail about the postsale strategy, which is actually where our relationship truly begins. This is what we've promised the world, and now it's time to overdeliver on our promise!

Creating Your Buyer's Journey

If you're completely new to sales, perhaps your buyer's journey can easily fit into the same process that works for me. If that's the case, please feel free to use the one I've laid out for you, and if you find ways to improve it, I'd love to hear about them. If you've been selling for a while and don't have an ideal buyer's journey documented, I suggest that you take a few minutes and think of the deal you're most proud of winning. It's one of those nail-biters that you weren't sure you were going to win, but you pulled out all the stops and really convinced the buyer that you, your organization, and your product or service are the absolute best solution and partner for them and their company. If you take time to answer the following questions, I believe you'll be able to replicate your efforts in future business deals, and it will help you win more often!

Here are a few questions to help you think through that one special deal that you may have won:

- What was different about that sale compared to your other ones?
- Can you trace back all your steps from beginning to the close? What were they?
- How did you set the first meeting?
- What did you uncover that made the customer want to meet with you again?
- What made you stand out from everyone else?
- Why did the customer buy from you?
- What would you have done better if you could do it all over again?

I believe that if you have clear answers to the above questions, you'll be better equipped to dominate your future opportunities. Sales is not magic; it's a science and a proven process that works for people who follow it. Unfortunately, many sales professionals simply react to opportunities. They allow the customer to tell them what they need, and they sell it to them without really adding anything to the buyer's journey or the buyer's experience. I call those people order takers, not sales professionals. I'm not saying that it's bad to be an order taker, because there are many clients who know exactly what they want to buy. Most companies have established major accounts who've been sold on a solution or a product, and when they need something new from time to time, they call in and request it. We really do need order takers; however, for our purposes, I'm talking about sales professionals—the people who develop a connection out of nothing and then build it to become a mutually beneficial relationship for years to come. These are the people who have a strong understanding of the challenges their customers face in the marketplace, and they take time to learn how to help these organizations increase their revenues. Then they align their products and services with their prospective buyer's goals, values, and initiatives to create an incredible win-win scenario.

As we move forward to speaking about the buyer's journey, you may find it useful to approach it from a standpoint of "How can I help my client generate more revenues with my products and services?" By keeping this type of curiosity at the forefront, you will be genuinely curious and more interested in helping your client than getting the deal. This is the mind-set I'm asking you to uphold as we move to the next section. It will help you create the long-lasting relationships most of us dream of having.

Create Your Buyer's Journey

Creating your buyer's journey is similar to setting the GPS for your week. It allows you to be a confident leader for your buyer because if you have an established plan for their journey, you're going to be better equipped to set the vision for them and guide them through the confusing and sometimes tedious process of acquiring a new product or service. In addition, if you do it correctly, you will create a strong, long-lasting relationship.

Do you currently have a buyer's journey that you always follow? If you do, are you winning most of the opportunities that you're currently involved with or are there areas that need improvement within your process?

Write out your ideal buyer's journey. Here are some questions to help you think through your buyer's journey:

- How will I attract my clients?
  - » Who can refer me to new opportunities?
  - » Where can I meet a potential client?
  - » What groups would they be in?
  - » What will I say on a cold call? Phone call?

- What do I want to find out when meeting a potential client?
  - » Their challenges?
  - » Their goals?
  - » What's holding them up?
  - » What are their top competitors doing better than them?

- What will my analysis consist of? List out three to five things you want to analyze.

- What will my validation meeting be like? What is my goal for the validation?

- How can I effectively ask for the business?

- Am I focusing on the sale or the client?

- How does my ideal buyer's journey match up to what I actually do?

- What can I change to improve my process immediately?

- What do I do differently in the sales process when I win deals versus when I lose (besides pricing)?

- What can I do to better stand out from my competition?

- If I were my client, why would I buy from me?

CHAPTER 5
The Secret to Not Get Rejected

Our words have the power to destroy and the
power to build up.
-Proverbs 12:6

When I first started in sales, my manager and I were having a conversation after he trained me on our products. He said, "Eric, today you're going to go cold-calling."

I remember hearing those words and not having a clue of what they meant. I looked at him and asked, "What's cold-calling?"

He explained that cold-calling means to stop by organizations to introduce myself, find the right contact person, and try to schedule a meeting with them. I thought it sounded pretty simple and went out there like the young, motivated, recently separated marine that I was. Because I realized that I asked a pretty dumb question about cold-calling, I was too uncomfortable to ask other "dumb" questions, like the one that came to mind as soon as I left the office. I got into my car, and the first thought that hit me was, *Who the hell buys a copier?* Since I'd never worked in an office environment before, I had no idea who bought or used copiers. See what I mean by "dumb question"? So I drove around, and a light bulb went off as I was passing a print shop where they made copies for people.

I parked my car and walked into that shop. This print shop had copy machines the length of a pickup truck, and I automatically thought it was exactly what I needed to find. The man came up to me, and after a quick introduction, he started asking me questions about my products, which I had no real answers for. Remember—my job was to schedule a meeting, and then I was going to bring in my manager to learn how to conduct a successful meeting. Needless to say, this gentleman had been in the printing business for a long time, and he knew way more about copiers than I knew at that time in my career. He also knew that the brand I sold did not have a product for a print shop environment. To offer a comparison, this situation was the same as if I had been speaking with a car mechanic about letting me fix his car when I knew nothing about cars and was missing all the tools to make his car run properly!

I got my butt handed to me that day! I was completely unprepared, had no idea what was important to a print shop, and was schooled by a person who knew way more than I did about my own business. I walked out of there with my tail between my legs and an amazing lesson. I learned that I needed to have a clearer understanding of what I wanted to speak with people about when I approached them.

I can confidently say that the same principle applies today. Knowing what we want to say before saying it allows for our talk track to be natural. Whether we're at a networking event, making phone calls, sending emails, or in a social setting, we should have a plan for when people ask us, "What do you do?" Let me ask you, What do you do? How would you answer that question? Now, for the fun of it, ask your coworkers the same question. I think you'll find that everyone has a different answer, and most of them will stumble for a few seconds before being clear. The other mistake they'll make is that they will actually tell you what they do! For example, if someone asked me, "What do *you* do?" I could say, "I train people in sales and leadership." However, that doesn't generate much interest. A more effective answer would be "I help organizations grow their revenues and retain amazing people." Answering that way always generates a follow-up question and allows us to start a conversation. I believe that when people ask, "What do you do?" they mainly want to know what you can do for them. Even if they genuinely want to know what you do, changing that question into "What can I do for them?" allows you to formulate your answer in a way that positions you to be interesting to them.

In this chapter, I'm going to give you some simple talk tracks and ice breakers that work for me. The important part to understand is that this is what works for me, and it will not always work for everyone. I'm asking you to really develop your talk tracks to fit your style and personality. Otherwise, it will be difficult for you to appear genuine when prospecting for new business, and it may prevent you from getting in front of the right people. It's very important that you find your comfort level where you can speak naturally and fluently when reaching out to potential clients. It's my intention to provide you with samples that you can build on to increase your success rate.

Ready? Here we go!

Cold-Calling in Person

Many people have a negative association with cold-calling door-to-door. Are you one of them? I believe it's because we dislike rejection and that uncomfortable feeling of walking into an unknown place to speak with a stranger. How creepy does that sound? It's amazing how as children we're taught to "never talk to strangers," and now, as adults in a sales role, our success depends on talking to strangers! Funny how life works sometimes. Can you see why some people may have a negative reaction to it? I can, and I completely understand how you feel if you don't like doing it either. Unfortunately, there is no escaping it if you want to be successful in sales. It's a part of the deal; you must go out there and find opportunities.

What I can help you with, before giving you the talk track, is encouraging you to think differently about making cold calls. The reason it's so important is because when you walk into a business, if your smile is not genuine, and the truth is you don't want to be there, people will see right through you and will not want to meet with you. It's imperative that we shift our perception of cold-calling to help make it feel more enjoyable, not just make it *seem* like it's enjoyable in front of others. I think if you're in a sales role, you absolutely love people. You enjoy speaking with them and helping others. Is that a correct assumption?

If my assumption is correct, let me suggest that instead of thinking, *I have to go cold-calling today,* we shift our thought to, *I get to go cold-calling today! Woohoo!* What else would you rather be doing? If you love people and enjoy speaking with them, how awesome is a career where you can just leave the office whenever you want and go talk to amazing people in your city? When I walk past administrative people who have to be in the office eight hours a day, looking at their computer screens and analyzing reports, I feel grateful for the opportunity to have the freedom to roam my marketplace like a lion in a safari! That's the mentality I'm asking you to possess when you're out there prospecting and searching for business. Feel the lion inside of you. Feel like this is your safari, and you're the king who gets to go wherever you please. Sound goofy? Well, what's the alternative? You can get a desk job and do that all day, but that doesn't sound that appealing to me. How about you? Cold-calling is a part of the deal. Unless you're in retail sales, you have to cold-call or your competitors will, and they will find the business that you decided not to call on today!

Before I move on, let me clear one thing up. What I said about administrative people is not meant to come off as degrading. As a matter of fact, our companies would not be able to function without them; they do so much to help the organization operate. I'm simply saying that if you're in sales, administration is probably not something you'd want to be doing. On the flip side of that coin, I realize that people who are in an administrative role look at salespeople and probably start feeling grateful that they get to sit in one place all day and don't have to go out and sell!

It's important to understand the goal of a cold call before diving into this section. Our main goal for the cold call is to schedule a meeting with the decision maker. If that person is not available, the secondary goal is to gather as much information as possible about their current situation.

Now, if you're excited about knocking on some doors and meeting strangers, here are two great things to keep in mind as you enter the business you're calling on.

1.   *The person at the front does not have the authority to buy from you, but they can tell you no.*

Be very selective about what you tell the person at the front desk. Remember that there are many people who can say things like "No, we're not interested," "That's not something the company would want," "They can't meet with you," and other negative things. But only a few can actually say yes to buying your product or service. Whatever you do, stay focused on your main goal of scheduling a meeting with the decision maker and do not give the person at the front desk a reason to turn you away.

You may be wondering why I said your main goal is to schedule a meeting with the decision maker. What else could your goal for a cold call be? I think many salespeople forget why they're cold-calling in the first place. I've been on many calls and have seen sales reps speak to the receptionist. They would say, "Hi, I'm Max from ABC Company. Can you please tell me who handles your *office equipment*? Or the person who is responsible for purchasing your *office equipment*?" You can just fill in a different product or service where I put *office equipment*, and it will apply to your industry.

Sometimes the receptionist says, "Amy Smith handles that. Here is her contact information. You can call her or email her directly."

The salesperson then says, "Thank you," and they walk out. I think it's because they feel like they got what they came for—the contact information!

If that sounds like the type of cold call you make, I'm asking you to tweak your goal from getting the business card of the contact person to scheduling an appointment with the decision maker. So, after the receptionist says, "Amy Smith handles that. Here is her information," we could respond with "Thank you so much. Can you please check to see if Amy is available right now?" If Amy is available, thank her for coming out and let her know that you appreciate her time. Then, go for scheduling a meeting with her, or see if she has time to sit down with you right now. I'm willing to bet that if you're smiling, looking like you're having fun, and you've made a good first impression, Amy will sit down with you for a few minutes. In my experience, the person comes out to see me 10–15 percent of the time. When that happens, I've now skipped a whole step of going back to the office, making a phone call, and leaving a message with the hopes of scheduling a meeting.

If Amy is not available, I recommend that you gather as much information as possible from the receptionist. Find out

- who they currently use for your products or services,
- what they like or don't like,
- how long have they been using the company, and
- what the person up front loves about working at this company.

It's also a good idea to find other contact people within this organization. Think of who else might be the stakeholders or influencers in making a decision for your products or services. In the office equipment world, we encourage people to call on various levels and positions of an organization. We call on the owner/CEO, human resources, IT, finance, and marketing. By doing this, we're able to learn about the needs of different areas in the organization, and it also increases our chances of scheduling a meeting and starting a relationship.

If you've been used to calling on the same position within a company, it may be beneficial for you to take a few minutes and think about who else is involved in the decision-making process and who can greatly benefit from your product or service. Make a list of at least three more departments or people you can call on to maximize your chances of scheduling a meeting. You can write them in here:

1. _____
2. _____
3. _____
4. _____
5. _____

By having a clear vision of who you want to call on, you will be in a better position to clearly communicate with the receptionist when you walk in. I'll provide you with a talk track toward the end of this chapter, but first let's talk about not spilling your beans in the lobby!

2. *Don't spill your beans in the lobby.*

Many salespeople believe that they must communicate what they do to the person sitting at the front desk. They walk in and say, "Hi, I'm Max from ABC Company. I work with many companies in the area helping them reduce their costs on _____ and improving efficiency with_____. Our company is the number-one _____ in the region, and we have some of the best products for _____. Some of our products are really cool! They are_____."

Perhaps I embellished a little with that very enthusiastic cold call. It's a great example of Max spilling all his beans in the lobby. He literally told them everything he knows about his company and some of the products. Unfortunately, he told that information to the person who doesn't care, is not able to make a decision, and is able to turn him away and tell him that the company is not interested. When I say don't spill your beans in the lobby, I'm asking that you don't give the person up front any reason to say, "We're not interested in something like that."

It's important to understand that, most of the time, the person up front does not care much about your products or services. Their job is to direct people, answer calls, take care of administrative tasks, and—most important for a salesperson to understand—keep us out. That's why we often call them the gatekeepers. As a matter of fact, it's possible that they will get in trouble for letting you through to the decision maker. Unless the stars align and the decision maker is filling in for the receptionist while she's at lunch, or the receptionist has been told that the company is looking for the product or services you sell, flooding her with information will not be beneficial to your efforts. It will only fuel her with ways to say no to you. Remember what I said earlier: there are many people who can say no but only a few who can actually say yes and are able to buy from you. Find the ones who can buy and who have the ability to say yes, and then you'll have the right audience.

In my experience, keeping your talk track simple is the best way to go when cold-calling. My goal is to always engage the person in conversation and start building rapport with them. Remember it's not about our products or services. It's about scheduling a meeting with the right person within the organization.

Here is the cold call script that's been modified and proven to work pretty well in my line of B2B sales:

I walk in with a smile and high energy. This is extremely important because I want to build rapport quickly, and one of the quickest ways to do that is by being likeable. I usually start off with something humorous to say. For example: "Hi, I'm Eric. I was sent here to relieve you for the day! I'll sit at the desk, and you can go and enjoy your day! How does that sound?"

Most of the time, I get a laugh, and they say something like "I wish!" I usually respond with a question and ask them, "If you did get the rest of the day off, what would you do?" The reason I engage with them this way is because I want them to be in a happy mood when we're speaking. I believe that if I get them to think of all the fun they could have if they took the rest of the day off, they'll probably start feeling a little happier than they did before I spoke with them. It's a known fact that people may not always remember your name or what you said to them, but they will always remember how you made them feel. Our goal is to make people feel great! Therefore, I purposefully make them laugh and try to get them to think about something positive and pleasurable (like a day off) before I start asking them to help me.

Once we've established rapport and had a laugh together, they say, "How can I help you?" Or "Are you here to see someone?"

I reply with "Well, ma'am, I'm glad you asked. I'm kind of lost and would greatly appreciate it if you could help me out. Could you please tell me the best way to schedule a meeting with the CFO of the organization? By the way, who is that person?"

Usually they give me a name and number and tell me when the best time to call is. Once I get that information, I start asking about other stakeholders in the company. I usually ask who the CIO, CEO, COO, and director of marketing are. Once I see that they're getting uncomfortable, I ask, "Could you please check to see if the CFO is available?" I can either go down the list of contacts I just received, or I can ask, "Does the CFO have an administrative assistant?" If the answer is yes, I'll ask if they're available. If the answer is no, I ask for others from the list of people that they gave me. I will keep doing that until I get in front of someone or until they tell me that they'll get in trouble and ask me to leave. If that happens, I try to have one more laugh with the person and leave on a good note.

My goal on a cold call is to meet with someone who can make a decision or is involved in the process of buying my products or services. It's never to just get the contact information and leave. The important part to know is that, if we're not sent away by the receptionist and someone we ask for comes out to see us, we have to be at our best to impress them. Most likely, we've just interrupted their day, and they already view us as someone who's trying to sell them something. That's okay! Don't start worrying yet. The best C-level executives have a nice level of appreciation for a professional, intelligent salesperson. They know that their company is not able to run unless they sell something, and they understand the struggles salespeople face each day. I assure you many of them appreciate the hustle and the stop-in. One way to tell if you've impressed them is if they start asking you to interview with their company. In my opinion, that's one of the best compliments!

At this point, you're standing in front of the decision maker who was just asked to drop what they're doing and come out to speak with you. What do you say? I recommend that you stick to your goal of scheduling an appointment with that person, but now you have to present something specific that will benefit them and their organization. When I get in front of the vice president of human resources, I know that she's interested in everything related to people; they're her internal clients. I will not speak to her about the technological aspects of whatever I'm selling because I want to be specific to the things that are most important to her. I would say something like "Sarah, thank you so much for coming out to meet me. Is it possible for us to schedule a meeting, or do you have some time available to sit down with me right now?"

In the event that Sarah says, "Absolutely, I'll sit down with you right now," you can follow the initial meeting section in chapter 6. It will help guide you through that uncomfortable feeling of "What do I do now?"

Usually, Sarah will reply with "What is this regarding?" Or "What do you do?" (Remember this question?)

At this point, most salespeople make a crucial mistake. They say, "I'm with _____ company, and we help organizations acquire the best office technologies for the best price." Sometimes, they start listing the products they sell and the services they provide, and they end up opening the door to "We're all set in those departments, but give me your card, and I'll keep you in mind as things come up." Sound familiar?

Before I share my talk track for Sarah, I'm going to help you answer her question and position you in such a way that you're able to answer many of these types of questions in the future. As long as we understand that it's not about our products or services but what our products and services can do for the company we're calling on, we'll be in great shape. Here is what I mean.

Have you heard the one about the drill bit?

We have to remember that what we sell is completely different from what people buy! The drill bit is a great example of what we sell and what people buy being two different things. Let me ask you, How would you sell a drill bit? I ask this question when I facilitate sales training sessions, and most people start telling me about the durability of the drill bit, and the price point, and the cool sizes it comes in. People who are new to sales usually get very creative with their answers. However, we have to understand that no one really needs a drill bit because they like drill bits. The only reason people ever buy a drill bit is because they need to drill a hole! I recommend shifting our focus to the hole they're trying to make and not the drill bit itself. How would I sell a drill bit? First thing I would ask is "What kind of hole are you trying to make?"

In how many other areas of sales are we focusing on selling the drill bit when we should be focusing on the hole? I cannot emphasize this point enough, and it absolutely applies to everything we're selling today. Here is a quick chart to give you an example of what I'm talking about. I ask that you create something similar with your products and services. What they buy can also be a synonym for why they buy. Take a look at this chart.

What We Sell	What/Why They Buy
Sales Training	• increase revenues • attract more clients • retain great people
Car	• feel secure • look good • feel good • reliable travel • feel secure
Financial Services	• feel secure • give children an opportunity to go to college • have a plan for success
Copiers/Printers	• look professional • gain more business • improve workflow within the office • improve employee morale (ever want to kick your copier?)

One of the things that separates sales winners from an average sales rep is that they align their product with the customer's needs. My goal is to show you that if you understand why the VP of HR (or whoever came out to see you on the cold call) would be interested in your product or service, and you're able to translate that into an emotional attachment for them, you will have a greater chance of securing your meeting and closing the sale.

You may find it beneficial to create your own chart on a separate sheet of paper and write out your products and services on the left side and the reasons people buy them on the right side. See if you can come up with at least five reasons for each product or service. Tackle it from the eyes of the end user, decision maker, finance person, technology person, parent, doctor, child, woman, man ... whoever may be able to buy what you're selling! It may also help to answer the following questions when doing this exercise:

- How will my product or service improve their situation?
- Why do they need my product or service?
- What happens when my product or service is not working?

Here is an example of what I'm talking about. I left blank spaces for you to fill in with your products and services. Good luck!

What We Sell	What/Why They Buy
Document Management Software	Store and Find any document quickly Security of sensitive information Improve efficiency Stay compliant

How do you feel about your list? Were you able to come up with multiple reasons why someone would want to buy your product or service? We must be prepared to explain to our audience the why that best applies to them. For example, if I want to use "security of sensitive documents" as my reason for scheduling the meeting, I would probably focus on the HR and IT departments because they're the ones who often care more about keeping information secure than others would. If you haven't done so yet, I strongly encourage you to create your list and write down as many things as you can. It may be a good idea to work with your team members on this because they will all have a slightly different perspective and will add valuable ideas to this exercise.

Cold Call Scenarios

Now that we understand the difference between what we sell and what people actually buy, we can create a talk track that will help us focus on our client's needs instead of our products and services. This will help us schedule more meetings with the right people. Here is what my talk track would be if I was selling document management software and wanted to schedule a meeting with the VP of human resources, Sarah Smith, via an in-person cold call.

Me: Good morning! How are you today?
Receptionist: I'm okay. How can I help you?
Me: Is Sarah Smith available?
Receptionist: Is she expecting you?
Me: I don't think so. Can you please ask her if she has a few minutes?
Receptionist: What's this regarding?
Me: I'm trying to schedule a meeting with her.
Receptionist: About?
Me: Helping her team be more productive.

The Receptionist Stops You

It would be nice if we were able to get through to the decision maker on every cold call; however, in reality, there will be many times when the receptionist will prevent that from happening. They will say things like this:

- We're not interested,
- She doesn't see people without an appointment.
- Give me your card, and I'll make sure to give it to Sarah.
- If Sarah is interested, she will call you.

In those cases, you comply with the receptionist and do your best to make her your friend. If the opportunity is worth pursuing, make sure to research the company during your research time. Learn as much as you can about Sarah, their industry, and her company and think of creative ways your product or service may help Sarah. Once you have an idea, read the breakthrough cold call section in chapter 6 to help you craft and convey your idea to Sarah.

Sarah Is Not Available

If Sarah is not available, I would see if she has an assistant who handles her calendar. If she doesn't have an assistant and no one is able to schedule this meeting with her, I would turn it into an intentional stop-in where I would have a letter written to Sarah asking for an appointment. We will dive deeper into the intentional stop-in in chapter 6.

Sarah Comes out to See You

If Sarah comes out, our conversation would go like this:

Me: Thank you so much for coming out to meet with me, Sarah. How are you today? (I always ask a question to get the other person engaged in a conversation.)
Sarah: I'm fine. What can I help you with?

Me: I'm hoping to schedule a brief introduction meeting with you. Do you have some time for us to sit down right now? Or would you prefer to schedule for later in the week?

Sarah: I'd love to sit down right now! (Yeah right! Don't you wish it was that easy?)

Sarah would really say: What's this regarding?

Me: The reason I wanted to meet with you is because other HR professionals found tremendous benefits in striving to become more efficient with their onboarding processes. I work with (name a competitor), and we've helped them automate some time-consuming functions for their staff. One thing I've seen over and over again, after partnering with our organization, is a tremendous boost in people's morale, not to mention a wonderful return on investment. Given an opportunity and all the resources, how would you improve your onboarding process?

Option 1

Sarah: Well, we haven't really thought about that. I think I'd like to learn more.

Me: That's wonderful! Do you have some time for us to sit down right now or should we schedule a time for later this week?

If Sarah doesn't have time right now, I would ask for her to look at her calendar and give her a few dates as options to meet.

Me: I completely understand. What does your schedule look like tomorrow at 2:00 p.m. or Friday in the morning?

If Sarah is available, we would proceed to the introduction meeting step of our buyer's journey.

Option 2

Sarah: Thank you for stopping in. That's not something we're interested in at this moment.

Me: Thank you, Sarah. I appreciate that feedback. May I ask what your onboarding process looks like right now?

I would want to understand what Sarah is currently doing and if she's truly not interested because they're operating efficiently or if she's not interested because I didn't do a good job at articulating the benefits to her company. Both can be valid, and if it's the latter one, I would need to work on my talk track and practice delivering it to my coworkers so that I can improve my skill set.

In reality, not everyone is going to be interested in our services at the time we meet with them. However, if we do a good job learning about their current situation and when they may be in the market, we will be in a better position to contact them at that time. This will also give us time to build a relationship with that person in the meantime.

I Spoke in Terms of What They Buy, Not What I Was Selling

I want to emphasize the fact that I never mentioned document management software or the name of the product and kept my focus on improving efficiency and boosting morale for her employees. The reason I intentionally stay away from speaking about products during a cold call is because I'm really not sure if my product will be able to help this organization at this stage of the game.

Imagine a scenario when you go see a doctor for knee pain, and as soon as you meet them, without asking you why you're there, they give you a pill and say, "You're in luck! This is the best medicine for headaches on the market." That could absolutely be the best medicine (product or service) out there, but it doesn't mean that it will be a good fit for you.

I'm suggesting that we, in sales, be more like doctors. Evaluate the customer, ask them everything possible about their current condition, understand the history of how they got to this point and what types of things they want to achieve, and know the challenges that are preventing them from achieving those things before talking about any products. This philosophy has helped my team greatly. Oftentimes, we hear our clients praise us for really wanting to understand their environment and not just trying to sell them something.

B2C Sales

Before I move on to prospecting via phone, I want to address the business to consumer (B2C) salespeople who knock on people's homes to sell them something. Unfortunately for me, I've never had an opportunity to knock on people's homes to present a product or service, and I have the utmost respect for you if that's your role. I hope you understand that when I write about cold-calling or selling, my experience is in business-to-business sales. With that said, I always like to listen to the people who knock on my door and really give them an opportunity to sell me their product or service because I know how hard and uncomfortable their job can be. Needless to say, it drives my wife crazy when I let every book-selling, energy-costs-reducing, lawn-mowing, fundraising, and cookie-selling salesperson into the house to give them a shot! I want to share with you what I think works best. I hope it may give you an idea or two as you continue to sell door-to-door.

The first thing I recommend is that you act as if your company and product is the absolute best in the world. As a matter of fact, if you don't really believe that your company or product is the best, you should try to find another job. Never sell a product that you don't believe in because it comes across as unauthentic, and people will see right through that.

Realize that you most likely caught them at an inconvenient time of the day and they don't want to be sold anything, especially at their home. Therefore, try to be excited and possess high, positive energy when people come to the door. Smile as if you just ate a banana sideways! It's amazing how contagious a wonderful smile and a little bit of positive energy can be.

Start off by asking if this is a good time to introduce your company or if it would be better to schedule a meeting with them at a later date and time. This shows that you respect their time, and most likely, they will end up asking you what it is you'd like to speak about anyway. Once they ask, you've now allowed them to initiate the conversation, and now you're in the position of answering their question instead of pitching a product or service to someone who may not be interested.

Once you've been given the opportunity to present, start off with a question. If you're selling solar panels, you may want to start off with "Sir/ma'am, when is the last time you had your energy bill evaluated?" Wait for their response, and if they say, "Never" or "A long time ago," you can continue with "The reason I ask is because we specialize in helping people reduce their energy expenses while promoting green energy and helping our clients increase the value of their homes (only if this is a true statement). On average, our clients have saved up to $xxx per month, and I believe there is a good chance we can help you realize the same type of savings. Are you available this Wednesday at 7:00 p.m. to explore ways you may be able to improve your current situation?" Notice that there is no pitch about panels or my company, there is no mention of features for my products, and I didn't start off by telling them what I'm selling. It's important to ask a question because it initiates a conversation and allows us, as sellers, to gain better insight into the person's thoughts before selling anything.

Conclusion

There have been times when I have had to force myself to cold-call. Many days, I wanted to *feel like* doing it before going out there, and unfortunately that feeling never came. So I found other busywork to do during those times. Looking back now, I realize that I ended up wasting a ton of time, and possibly losing opportunities, because I didn't *feel like* cold calling. It's a funny thing about feelings. The world doesn't stop when we wait to feel like we want to do something. The best thing we can do for ourselves, as sales professionals, is make a weekly commitment to an amount of cold calls we're going to make—and stay committed to our commitment. We must develop a discipline to do the moneymaking activities and stick to our discipline, no matter how we feel!

For many people, cold-calling is the toughest part of being in sales. I truly believe it's due to rejection. My goal for this chapter was to help you minimize the rejections while maximizing your success rate during the call. So, to recap, how do we do that?

1. Remember that the person at the front (receptionist) does not have the authority to buy from you, but they are able to tell you no. We must be very respectful, nice, and courteous to them. But avoid telling them about what we can do for the company; remember to not spill your beans in the lobby. That can open the door to them saying, "We're not interested in that." Instead, just ask for the person who is able to make a decision and buy.

2. Have and understand your goal for each cold call. The goal is not to sell them something on a cold call. The goal is to schedule a meeting with the right person. I found it works best if I aim for scheduling a meeting while I'm there and having the right person sit down with me for a meeting on the spot. However, if the person is not available to meet at this time, the second best is to schedule the meeting for a future date before leaving the cold call.

3. Have fun! People love to be around people who are having fun. Enjoy your experience, act like you want to be there, and believe that you have the best product or service to greatly benefit the organization you're visiting.

Prepare for Cold Calls

Cold-calling in person is one of those things that successful salespeople should learn to love. Initially, it's an uncomfortable feeling to walk into a business and start a conversation with complete strangers who are annoyed that you walked in. However, there was a time in your life when driving, talking to someone of the opposite sex, and conducting your very first sales meeting were uncomfortable as well. With time, you were able to overcome that feeling, and you're probably very comfortable with doing at least two of the three things today. Your cold-calling skills will develop in the same way. What's uncomfortable today will be second nature tomorrow if you make it a habit to do it on a regular basis.

Here are some questions to help you improve in the area of cold-calling and prospecting for new business.

- What's your goal for the cold call?
- How can you get excited about cold-calling?
- How do you respond when people ask you, "What do you do?"
- What can you do to improve your answer?
- What have you said during a cold call that made the person laugh? What's worked for you in the past?
- What do you say when you first walk in?
- Who are all the people you can call on with an organization? Write out their titles.
- What do you sell? How can what you sell help your potential client's organization?

CHAPTER 6
Prospecting Like a Pro

A conclusion is the place where you
get tired of thinking.
-Arthur Bloch

I believe the cold call is essential to grow our business and produce results. However, it's not the only method of effective initial contact with our potential clients. In this chapter, I'm going to share additional ways to generate leads and set initial meetings with potential clients. Before we move on, I want to clarify that I use cold-calling and prospecting interchangeably. To me, they both identify a way we look for new business. Cold-calling can be via phones or in person, and they both fall under prospecting.

Let's continue the conversation about our initial contact with the customer. The reason I'm spending so much time on covering the initial contact portion is because I believe that if you can get good at scheduling meetings with people who can buy, you will become extremely successful. Getting in front of the right people and opening an opportunity is the toughest part of the sales process in any organization. The rest is easy to learn. Here are some additional ways to help you open more doors, which will lead to creating better relationships!

I'm not sure that I ever met anyone who loves prospecting over the phone. Let's face it. No one likes telemarketers or being on the receiving end of a cold call. People have gatekeepers to keep us out, and even though people love to shop and buy new things, they hate being sold to. Those do not sound like great odds for being able to schedule a meeting; therefore, it's easy for us to become discouraged when prospecting over the phone. I completely understand the frustration, uncertainty, discouragement, and roadblocks that stand in your way as sales professionals when prospecting over the phone. I also understand the fact that most organizations measure salespeople's levels of performance by their activity levels, which makes prospecting over the phones even worse. Let me explain what I'm talking about.

When we're measured by our activity levels, we tend to focus on the amount of activity instead of the quality of it. Let's face it. We all know that the sales manager will look through the CRM at some point during the week to make sure that their reps are making the amount of calls they're required to make. The reason they do that is because the sales managers are meeting with their VPs and the president of the company on a weekly basis to discuss activity levels of their team members. That's the way they're being managed and coached. It's easy for a VP-level person to look at the spreadsheet, see that John only made fifty calls for the week, and automatically assume that the reason John's sales are low is because of the low activity levels.

There may be some truth to that; however, it does not paint the whole picture. Unfortunately for John, the VP will probably call John's manager, and the manager will have a conversation with John about making more calls. Does that sound familiar? This is the same old-school philosophy of sales being a numbers game. I totally agree that we increase our chances of success when we speak with more people; however, if we're calling one hundred people per week and not scheduling a single meeting, the plan to call another hundred to be successful is just plain naïve and silly!

Care More about Helping Your Clients

Sales is about wanting to help people achieve better results, and it's about connecting with people. It's not about forcing a product on someone just because that's what you happen to be selling at the moment. I'll give you an example where a salesperson wanted to sell me their product even though it wasn't the right thing for my family. I've never forgotten that and will never buy anything from that person in the future. Your clients are the same way; they want to buy from someone who is genuinely interested in helping them achieve their desired result, not the salesperson's. Before our children were born, my wife, Julia, and I were both in sales. She was in pharmaceutical sales, and I was selling copiers. We were both doing well financially, and life was great, considering the fact that we were twenty-five and twenty-six years old. After paying all of our monthly expenses, traveling, partying, and shopping, we were still left with about $2,000 per month to save or invest for our future together. I met a "financial planner" in my BNI group and thought it would be amazing to work with someone who could help us create our financial goals and design a plan for us to follow. When we sat down with this woman, she opened her computer software and asked us questions about our financial situation. She asked us to tell her how much money we made, what we spent, and what we had left over at the end of the month. Magically, she came up with a great solution. She wanted us to buy an insurance policy that cost … ready for this? Two thousand dollars per month! Isn't it amazing how the stars aligned for her? The biggest turnoff was that she couldn't care less about our goals. I knew this because she didn't ask a single question about what we wanted to achieve in the future; she only wanted to sell her product. At least that's how it felt to us. As you have probably already guessed, we ended up not hiring her as our financial planner!

The lesson I learned through that experience was that if I wanted to be successful in sales, I needed to care more about helping people than I cared about my commission. If we help people improve their situation, they will pay us for it, and we will benefit financially. However, when we focus more on our financial gain than we do on helping people, we end up losing. If we want to be successful in sales, we must be authentic and genuinely curious about finding the best solution for our potential clients. The only way we can ever do that is by understanding their business, their challenges, their competition, their customers, and their goals.

Cold-Calling via Phones

Unfortunately, it can be very challenging to understand an organization prior to making a call to them when we're tasked with making hundreds of calls. What ends up happening is that we call on companies that we know nothing about, and we try to tell them about our product or service, which they may or may not need.

Sometimes, however, this shortsighted approach works. We actually end up scheduling a meeting this way because the person we called on happens to be in the market and is currently shopping for what we're selling. Awesome! Right? Nope, unfortunately not. What happens in those situations is that we end up in bidding wars and oftentimes blindly give them a proposal (of course they need three to make a decision) before really understanding their current situation or their goals for the future. Those opportunities seldom turn into win-win scenarios. I actually began telling people that I was not going to be able to provide them with a proposal in those situations. You know what? It liberated me! If people weren't willing to meet with me and have an intelligent conversation, I was not going to take the time to give them a proposal or send them information with the hopes that they would call me. I learned early on that they rarely, if ever, call.

Do the Work before Making the Call

If you want to greatly improve your chances of scheduling more meetings when making calls, you will have to research the company and person you want to contact prior to calling them. What I'm asking you to do is very simple; however, it's also difficult to do on a consistent basis. You may have to speak with your manager about this strategy and let them know that the volume of calls you're going to make will significantly drop. However, if this works for you the way it worked for me, your meeting numbers and sales numbers will greatly increase. Does this sound fair?

Joe Frazier, one of the greatest boxers, said, "Champions aren't made in the ring; they're simply recognized there." What Joe was talking about is all the preparation and hard work before the fight—those are the things responsible for making someone a champion, not the fight itself. The same goes for prospecting over the phones. If we want to be successful, we must know as much as possible about the client, their company, and some of the challenges within their industry before making the call.

The strategy that best worked for me was to do my research on Sunday evenings. This is what I discussed in chapter 3 about having a weekly plan. I would pick out ten companies that I wanted to call on during the week and gather as much information as possible. I wanted to know answers to the following questions:

- What's their mission, vision, and purpose?
- What do they do?
- Who are their competitors?
- Are they in the news?
- Who are the CEO, CFO, director of IT, VP of marketing, VP of HR, director of administration?
- What is each person's background?
- What groups are they in?
- What school did they attend?
- Are they prior-service military? What branch?

Sometimes it was easy to gather this information, and other times it was more difficult. However, the more I knew before making the call, the better equipped I was to make my talk track more customized and appealing to the individual I was calling on. Most people call on an organization and just start firing off all the things they do and how they can help someone generally. Remember how we shouldn't spill all the beans in the lobby? The same applies to the phone. The times I had success on the phones was when I called and had a specific way to help an organization.

Today, most people receive a call that sounds like this: "Hi, I'm (insert name) with (insert name of company). We specialize in helping companies like yours or (insert specific industry) with reducing their costs on (insert product or service). Do you have some time available to learn more?" If it's not exactly like that, it's definitely a variation of it. The reason it has to be general is because most sales reps have not done the research about the company or the person they just called. They're simply dialing to achieve the right amount of calls so they can avoid the "lack of activity" conversation with their manager on Monday morning. I can't say that I blame them!

Now imagine being the CEO or an owner of a company and receiving a call like this:

Me: Hi, Stacy. How are you doing today?

Stacy: Okay.

Me: I'm calling with the hopes of scheduling a brief introduction meeting with you.

Stacy: What's this in regard to?

Me: I recently read an article about your initiatives to hire more people from your community. Is that still on your agenda?

Stacy: Yes.

Me: Fantastic. I think what you're doing is absolutely amazing. Thank you! The reason I'd like to meet with you is because we have a few ways to help organizations seamlessly onboard new employees. What I'd like to speak with you about will tremendously reduce the amount of time your staff takes to process all the paperwork associated with a new hire and will give you a way to access all of their information within seconds! Do you have some time this Wednesday or Thursday for us to get together?

Most likely, Stacy will say yes in this situation. However, if she said no, I would then make a reference to another organization I may have helped with a similar project. I would reassure her that I can be a great resource and that she has absolutely nothing to lose and much to gain by meeting with me.

The only way to know about the people we're calling on is to intentionally try to learn about them. Use tools like LinkedIn, Google, Facebook, Twitter, and any other social media platform that may have been created since I wrote this book to your advantage. There is tons of information available to give you a glimpse of what the other person enjoys, their education, their work history, their presence in the news, and their interests. If the information is out there, try to gather as much as possible in order to be more effective with your call. The successful sales professionals take their time and energy to understand the individuals they're trying to meet with. They realize that connecting with others is the key to success, and they try to find common ground or learn as much as possible about the other person. My mentor, John Maxwell, says, "People don't care how much you know until they know how much you care." One way people know that you care is when they see you taking time to learn about them. I'm asking that you learn as much as possible about the person you want to meet with prior to calling them. I guarantee that you will be more effective on the call if you adopt this approach.

The Breakthrough Cold Call

I remember receiving a postcard in the mail. It was from a local car dealership, and it had my name on it, with a picture of a newer version of my car. In addition, it stated that they would give 125 percent of my current car's value as a trade-in. I was intrigued by that level of detail and decided to research various technologies and software packages that can personalize marketing materials that way. Once I found the solution, I reached out to a university that hadn't been returning my calls. The difference this time was that instead of calling on IT, I called the person who was responsible for recruiting new students. When I got a few minutes with her, I said, "I have a way to improve your recruiting efforts and attract students to the university. Can we sit down for a few minutes?" Guess what? We sat down! I learned a great deal about their process and ultimately presented a solution with this software package that customized a letter to the potential students, with pictures of the things they were interested in, written just for them and their parents. It was an in-depth solution that we don't need to get into here, but it's important to know how I created that opportunity. It was because I spoke about the things *they wanted to accomplish*—an increase in student population and ultimately an increase in revenues.

I hope I've articulated this point well and you realize why it's so important to understand the what and why behind your client's buying decisions. I assure you that if you have a clear understanding of this, you will be way better equipped to improve your client's current situation, align your products and services to best benefit them, create a win-win solution, and therefore close more sales.

Intentional Stop-In

Sometimes, no matter how many times we try to call a person, they never seem to be available for a phone conversation. Don't worry. It happens to the best of us. If you've left a few messages and have not received a call back, it may be a good idea to intentionally stop in. The reason I say "intentionally" is because this stop-in is way more than just a cold call, as we spoke about before. The intentional stop-in will be directed, specific, and targeted to the one person you've been attempting to schedule a meeting with. It should be scheduled in your calendar like a standing appointment and requires some creative planning to execute properly. The goal for this stop-in is to stand out from all the other salespeople who may be calling on this organization and to ultimately meet with the person who's been tough for you to reach.

I remember selling copiers with a good friend, Mike Cronin. Mike was also a marine and was very successful at selling and connecting with his clients. If Mike was involved, you could rest assured that the customer was going to be taken care of and that Mike would have an amazing relationship where everyone in the office knew him, liked him, and trusted him. Me being a newer sales rep at the time, I remember being stuck trying to schedule a meeting with a CFO of a company, and I went to Mike for some advice. I asked what he would do in this situation. He told me a story about a time he was stuck and how he was able to get the meeting because of the intentional stop-in (though that's not what he called it).

As I recall, Mike was calling on a decision maker for months without a single returned call. After a while, he stopped in at the location and made friends with the person who manned the front desk. Some of you in sales would call her the magical gatekeeper! Through their conversation, Mike found out that the person he'd been calling on just returned from maternity leave. He quickly went out, bought a pair of baby shoes, and wrote a note that said, "I'm just trying to get my foot in the door. Will you please give me ten minutes of your time?" Mike attached this note along with a business card to one of the baby shoes and asked the front desk person to deliver it to the decision maker.

You can probably guess that Mike was able to schedule the meeting, and they bought technology from Mike for years after that stop-in.

The greatest lesson from Mike's story is that he was extremely thoughtful, intentional, and creative. He spoke to a new mother with a note attached to a baby shoe! Isn't that amazing intuition? He connected with her on a level that most other sales reps weren't able to do, and he stood out from the rest. That's what intentional stop-ins are all about; they have to be thoughtful and targeted to the person you're trying to meet with in order to achieve the same results that Mike achieved.

Are you thinking of that one person who hasn't been returning your calls? What do you know about them? It's so easy to learn about people these days, isn't it? Many of them are on social media, which makes our lives way easier, but for the ones who aren't, we can do what Mike did and go talk with the gatekeeper.

What can you do this week to stand out from the crowd and get a few steps closer to penetrating that account you always wanted? If you have some ideas, right now would be a great time to pause reading and get those ideas on to your calendar while they're still fresh! Make sure that your stop-in is unique. Dropping by with a box of doughnuts is nice, but everyone does that! What can you do that will make that person smile unexpectedly? When you're able to answer that question, you will tremendously increase your chances of scheduling a meeting with the person who's been ignoring you. I promise!

Email

Many salespeople try to schedule their first appointment via email. Though I don't fully agree with that approach, I think if done in a creative enough way, we can be successful with it. I remember calling on the CFO of the National Rifle Association (NRA). I tried every which way to reach him and left many messages with no luck of ever receiving a call back. I can't really blame him; I most likely wasn't appealing or persuasive enough for him to call me back.

Before I finish this story, please take note of one thing. When something is not working for you, it's best to always—and I mean *always*—blame yourself for the result. This is effective because we cannot change anyone else; we can only change ourselves and how we handle the situation in front of us. Okay, back to the NRA. Since the voice mails and messages with the administrative assistant weren't getting the results I was expecting, I decided to send him an email. If you don't have the person's email, you can call the organization and ask for it. I knew that my email had to be short, direct, and amusing enough for him to stop what he was doing and look at it. This is what I came up with:

The subject line: "Rick, I have a quick question for you."

The body of the email said, "How does a prior-service marine go about scheduling a brief introduction meeting with the CFO of the NRA?"

That was my whole email! Within minutes, I received a reply from him. His email started off with "Great email, Eric." Then he said, "What does your company do?" I wish I could tell you that I was able to secure the appointment with him, but I did not! I believe it's because I made the classic mistake that I spoke about in the "what we sell versus what they buy" section and wrote back with a description of our services. In hindsight, I should have concentrated more on how the NRA would benefit by partnering with someone like us.

Though I did not secure a meeting, I was able to get his attention because my email was different from most other ones that he probably receives. I've seen sales professionals write an introductory email as if they're writing a book. They go on and on about their products and services and what they can do for the organization. If you have a habit of that, please stop and reevaluate the results you're actually getting from those types of emails. I'm guessing not really good ones. That's because people aren't reading them. I know I'm not. Think about it this way: If you write everything about your products and services and email it to a potential client, you've given them enough information to tell you they're not interested at this time but to stay in touch. Sound familiar? It also shows that you don't have much consideration for their time. Just because you have all day to think of clever things to say about your products or services and then articulate that in your email doesn't mean that the client has the time to read all of that.

When writing your email to schedule an introduction meeting, remember to keep it as short as possible, make it funny, let it be specific to the person you're writing to, and stay on message. Your initial email should not be a sales pitch for your products or service. It should be focused only on getting the person to agree to meet with you. So how do we do this? How do we get the person to meet with us if they've never met us before and have been ignoring our voice mails? I believe that our chances of scheduling a meeting greatly improve if we have done some research on the company and the person prior to hitting the Send button. Imagine how powerful you can make your email if you make it specific to them.

If I wanted to send an email to Sandy and I learned that Sandy is passionate about feeding the homeless, I would mention something about wanting to help her efforts—that aligning herself with people who have similar passions is one of the reasons she should meet with me. It's very important for me to note that I would say this only if I truly wanted to help and if it was authentic for me. Many people brag about their incredible skill of "faking it." I'm asking that you forget the "fake it till you make it" crap. It doesn't work. What works is authenticity, compassion, and empathy. People can feel it, and they will be more attracted to that. Show them that you cared enough to learn about them, and it will open your first door to meet with them. When I found out that one of my clients was into helping Toys for Tots, I immediately jumped in and volunteered my time. It wasn't to impress the client; it was because I'm passionate about Toys for Tots, giving less-fortunate children toys during Christmas, and helping marines look good in the community. Lucky for me, I was able to connect with the client more, and our relationship grew stronger.

Everything I described in the email section above can also apply if your initial contact is through LinkedIn. LinkedIn is an amazing tool to connect with people, understand their views, see where they've been, and read what others have to say about their work ethic and accomplishments. There are full chapters and books on how to use LinkedIn to grow your business. My purpose for bringing it to your attention is I want to make it clear that no matter what your channel of communication is, it's imperative that you do your research and make your first email, or any other contact, specific to that person. If you do decide to use LinkedIn as your initial method of contact, make sure your profile is amazing. Most people will look at your profile before responding to your message. Let them see how wonderful you are, and be sure to have some testimonials of the great work you did from your past clients and partners.

The key point to remember in any stage of the buyer's journey is to try to stand out from the rest. I recommend that we adopt the mentality of creating an amazing buyer's experience at every level. However, it's even more important to do if we're sending an email as an introduction. The customer can't see us and hasn't met us, and—let's face it—we're kind of intruding, right? At least in their minds we are, and what they think will either give us the green light to proceed to a meeting or hit the Delete button without us ever knowing. If you're writing that email, ask yourself one question before sending it: "Would I meet with me if I received this email?" If the answer is no, don't send it.

Before we move on to strategic partnerships, I want to caution you that sending an email or a message via LinkedIn could keep you in the comfort zone. It's easy to hit the Send button and not worry about people hanging up on you or telling you to "go screw yourself and to never call back." I get it. However, we must keep our cold-calling skills and techniques sharp at all times. There is nothing better than an in-person connection, so make sure you don't spend 100 percent of your prospecting time sending messages. It's nice to diversify!

Create a Strategic Alliance

When I was selling copiers in Baltimore, Maryland, I decided to join a BNI group for networking and leads-generation purposes. In my opinion, these types of groups are only as good as the people who belong to them. If there are people in multiple industries who call on the same position of person within a company as you do, then it could be beneficial to join that group. If you're in B2B sales and everyone else in the group is a residential real estate agent, mortgage broker, or plumber, this group may not be the best fit for you. My group was pretty good; they had more than a dozen other B2B sales professionals who were meeting with the same level of people I wanted to meet with. I especially hit it off with the local rep for ADP, a payroll-and-outsourced-HR company. His name was Ryan, and he was calling on C-level executives and small business owners, just like I was. We went out to lunch one day, and an idea hit me that generated more leads for me than anything else I'd been doing at that time. The best part about it was that this idea was going to greatly help both of us close more business and significantly benefit the customer as well. It was truly a win-win-win scenario, and not much more can beat that.

I asked Ryan what his average deal size was, and he told me that people usually signed up for around $120–$180 per month, if I remember correctly. I asked him if it would benefit him and his clients if they could get the first six months of his service at no cost. Can you imagine selling to a business and your product is completely free for the first six months? This wasn't a gimmick; they would literally receive a check in the amount equaling six months of their ADP invoice to make the payments from. Ryan looked at me and said, "Of course! That would be incredible." At that point, I shared my idea with him. I proposed that when he was in front of his customers to ask them what they were doing for their office technologies. Then he would tell them about our strategic alliance, where I would pay six months of their ADP invoice if they bought their office equipment from me. It was nothing for me to take $600–$800 out of my profit margins to gain a new client, but it was very intriguing for Ryan and his customers to receive such an amazing gift. This worked so well that Ryan introduced me to other ADP reps in the area, and I started doing the same thing with them. I literally had a sales team finding business for me. Why? Because I found a way for them to win more business.

Remember what Zig Ziglar said? "You can have anything in life that you want as long as you help enough other people get what they want." My idea for the ADP partnership was a classic example of this statement in action. Who can you align with today? How can you help them increase their business? One thing to keep in mind is that most people care mainly about themselves. It's unfortunate but true. That's why when we look at a group picture, we decide if it's good or not based solely on how we look in it. In reality, if you realize that people care mainly about themselves and you are able to place other people first, you will reap the rewards in the long run.

If you start implementing the morning routine and thinking time into your week, I suggest that you schedule some time to think about creating strategic alliances and unique ways to help others generate income before asking them to bring you into their accounts.

Conclusion

When we're prospecting, whether it's in person, over the phone, or through an email, a letter, LinkedIn, or a networking group, it's important to be creative, friendly, and memorable. I realize that there is a ton of noise in the marketplace and we're not the only people who are calling on our prospective decision makers. Many of our competitors are doing the same thing. It's tough to be 100 percent better than our competition, but I'm encouraging you to be 1 percent better in a hundred different ways. Taking the time to be creative, friendly, and memorable and placing the needs of your potential clients first will definitely make your prospecting at least 1 percent better than the rest of them, and it will help you create long-lasting relationships with your precious clients.

Get Hustling

I love seeing the pictures of lions and motivational words like "hustle" all over some salespeople's social media profiles. Many people seem to love the idea of it but don't understand that the true example of hustling is doing your research on Sunday night so that you can be more prepared for your week ahead. Not driving a Lambo. Want to hustle and be a beast in sales? Awesome! Let's start doing the things that most people won't do. Let's start doing the things that beasts and lions do. Are you ready to commit?

If you are, then take out your calendar right now and schedule time during the weekend to research people and companies you want to target next week. Make this a recurring event on a weekly basis, and stick with it no matter what. That's the first part to hustling.

- What ten companies can you target this week?
- What can you learn about them?
- Create a simple introduction email that you can reuse with minor tweaks.
- What would someone have to say to you on a telemarketing call for you to give them an opportunity?
- What can you say that will increase your chances of scheduling a meeting?
- What's your biggest roadblock when prospecting? How can you overcome it?
- Join a networking group and partner with people who meet with people you're targeting.

CHAPTER 7
The G.O.Y. Approach

This time, like all times, is a very good one, if
we but know what to do with it.
-Ralph Waldo Emerson

I can't really say that I remember my very first introduction meeting. Maybe it's because I was so terrible at it that my mind decided to block it out. All I can tell you is that the way I was initially taught to facilitate the introduction meeting was completely wrong. Unfortunately, I see way too many organizations and sales professionals still making the same mistakes today. It wasn't until I attended a three-day Dale Carnegie sales-training seminar that my approach became clear and I was able to adjust the way I facilitated the introduction meeting. This seminar changed the way I viewed sales, and I've been using everything I learned in that class ever since. I remember the instructor writing out the letters GOY on the board and asking everyone if we knew what they meant. No one had a clue, but once I learned what they meant, they became the pillars for the way I communicate with others and how I facilitate all introduction meetings, business and personal.

The letters GOY stood for "get over yourself"! The reason this was such a shock is because everything I'd learned about sales until that point in my life was all about selling our features, our benefits, our company, our service, my story … Do you see the conflict I was facing internally? This meant that I could no longer go in with a beautiful brochure, talking about my amazing company and describing how awesome my copier was because it could scan to email. (Scanning to email was very new back then.) It changed my life. I stopped going into meetings with my company profile or any kind of brochures, and the only thing I brought was my curiosity. I wanted to know and learn everything I could about the person and company I was meeting with. There was no secret agenda, just curiosity and the desire to develop a relationship.

In this chapter, I will lay out a guide for how to conduct an introduction meeting, and I'll give you some wonderful questions to ask so that you can get a clearer understanding of what your clients truly want to achieve and how you can be the one to help them.

Before I move on to the actual meeting, I want to first emphasize the fact that GOY works in all areas of our lives, not just in sales. Recently I had a conversation with a woman who was interviewing me to be her life coach. She was in her late forties, very outgoing, energetic, successful, pretty, and single. I couldn't believe that a woman like her would have a tough time finding a partner in her life and that she was struggling with loneliness. It was absolutely mind-boggling. During our conversation, I asked her why she believed she was single. She said that her friends thought it was because she was too picky. Naturally, I wanted to know the last thing her friends thought she was too picky about, and the list she laid out made me embarrassed to call myself a man. I could not believe some of the things guys were saying and doing on these dates. From wearing "mom jeans" and tennis shoes to wanting to split the check and everything in between. The one thing that stood out the most was when she told me that some of the men would not stop talking about themselves and their kids and they didn't seem that interested in learning about her. Come on, guys. We can do better than that! As I listened to her terrible-date stories, I realized just how much those three letters, GOY, can influence the outcome in any meeting situation. If those guys could have just gotten over themselves and learned about her, they might have increased their chances of developing a beautiful relationship. The same applies in sales. After all, isn't a first date just an introduction meeting? I believe it is.

If you spend any time around children, it's easy to see that they want to tell you everything about how awesome they are. They'll tell you how fast they run, how strong they are, what movie they saw, what their best friend did … However, they rarely ask us how we're doing. We understand that when children do it, it's a natural thing, and let's face it—they're only children and have not had the time to fully develop in that area. But when adults do it? It's a complete turnoff, and no one wants to be around people like that. Unfortunately, there are too many adults who never fully developed in that area.

I'm asking that you become more consciously aware of other people and the fact that they believe they are the most important people in the world. Know that they have many things to share about their lives and if you become the person to listen to them and be curious about them, they will want to be around you. In my experience, the salesperson who makes the client feel heard, understood, and important is the one who will most likely win the deal. I'm not talking about the ones who fake it till they make it. I'm speaking about the ones who genuinely want to help and are curious about the people they meet. They're authentic, and authenticity is the key.

When we meet with potential clients, they're interviewing us to see if we can help their organizations. If we're too busy talking about how awesome our companies are, how great we are, and how amazing our products are without getting to know them and their challenges, we will miss the boat and most likely will not be invited back to continue building the relationships. When I first became aware of the acronym GOY, I started writing it on the top left-hand corner of my notepad during my meetings with my potential clients. It helps me to remember to listen and ask more questions as opposed to speaking about myself. It helps me stay curious, with a childlike desire to learn everything I can from my experience.

Curiosity

Curiosity may have killed the cat, but where salespeople are concerned, lack of curiosity will kill your sale and any chance of building rapport with your potential clients. As children, our curiosity was never ending. Every question had a follow-up question, usually "Why?" I see it now with my little ones. If they don't fully understand something, they will stay curious until they get it. Children are relentless when it comes to learning and understanding new things, aren't they? I'm asking that we engage the same type of childlike curiosity with our prospects as our children do when they want to know why the sky is blue!

I recently joined Jenny, one of our sales professionals, on an introduction meeting with a nonprofit association in Virginia. I wasn't saying much because Jenny was doing a phenomenal job learning about the client and his needs. She asked incredible questions and really got the client engaged in the discussion. I could tell by observing his reaction that he was really being challenged mentally. It was awesome to see how Jenny's questions were generating thoughts he hadn't thought about before. Twenty minutes into the conversation, the gentleman said, "You guys are really different." Jenny and I were both caught off guard. We looked at each other and then asked him what he meant by that comment. He told us that we weren't the first vendor he'd met with and that no one else had asked those types of questions before, not even his current vendor. He said that the other companies came in with a brochure of their technologies and told him all about their products. What he liked about us was that we hadn't mentioned any products yet and were genuinely curious about his organization. Within a matter of three weeks, after conducting a thorough analysis, Jenny acquired a new customer!

Set Your Goals and Intention

On my journey of personal development, I've learned that setting a goal for every task helps me focus on the right things. You may find that it works the same for you. For example, when I'm reading a book and I start a new chapter, I look at the title and tell myself that my goal for this chapter is to take away three new ideas that will help me close more business. By stating that goal to myself, I prepare my mind to intentionally search for those ideas and keep my mind's eye open for the things that will help me. Setting small goals in every stage of our lives allows our minds to focus on the things we truly want to achieve. Why don't you give it a try the next time you're reading a book or going into an introduction meeting? You may absolutely love the new breakthrough, just as I did.

You may find it useful to visualize the meeting in your mind before ever meeting with the client. Understand what you want to accomplish if everything goes exactly the way you want it to go and keep that image as clear as possible. This will help you stay confident and focused on the outcome you want from your introduction meeting. In Jenny's situation, our goal was to schedule an analysis where we would be able to look at the way all the documents flow through this association, how much it costs them to print, and how many prints, copies, and scans they're producing. We made that very clear with each other before we ever met with the client. This helped Jenny ask the questions, which made the client want us to conduct an analysis just as much as we wanted to.

Icebreakers

Icebreakers are a wonderful way to start a conversation and get your clients speaking about something they're passionate about. I try to avoid starting the conversation about business, because I believe it's important to get to know one another first. At the end of the day, people will do business with people they know, like, and trust—or it will be because you have the cheapest price. We never want "the cheapest price" to be the reason for someone doing business with us, unless we're naturally the least expensive option, after building a relationship and being able to add tremendous value to our clients.

Before I continue to the introduction meeting, I want to emphasize that this is being written under the assumption that you've done your research before your meeting. If you're currently winging it, please reevaluate your approach. You can go back and reread the section about research in chapter 3. It's crucial before any first meeting and will greatly help you with your icebreakers. You've already worked hard to get the introduction meeting; why not come in extremely prepared and knowledgeable about the company and the person you're meeting with? At the very least, it will show that you took your time to learn about the most important person you're meeting with, the potential client!

I recommend starting the conversation by talking about something they've achieved, professionally and personally. It's amazing how many things we can find out about a person when we Google them. On the flip side, they're researching you as well, so make sure the live-stream video where you're professing your love for tequila on Saturday night is off the internet!

For many sales professionals, it's uncomfortable to start the conversation when they first meet the potential client. That's why they start talking about the weather and how lovely the office is to break the ice. Here are some alternative ways to break the ice and create a wonderful first impression:

"Hi, Amy. I learned that you've been here for twelve years and have moved through the ranks from a receptionist to the COO position. That's an incredible story! What drove you to achieve so much? Was that your goal from the very beginning?"

"Hi, John. I read that you retired from the marines. What's it like to be a marine for twenty-plus years? How does that relate to the job you're currently doing? What do you miss most about it?"

"Hi, Lisa. I read your blog about helping the homeless in our city. It was very eye-opening. How did you get involved with that? Why do you think you're so passionate about helping?"

"Hi, Vince. I noticed that you guys recently sponsored the Baltimore Ravens. Did you have anything to do with that? What do you think was the main reason behind the sponsorship? Are you a Ravens fan?"

If you're wondering how to get people to like you, it's simple. Like them first! I mean *truly* like them. Go out of your way to learn as much as possible about them, get them to speak about the things they're passionate about, and make them laugh. If you can do those things during your introduction meeting, I guarantee that they will like you.

Set the Agenda

After the icebreakers, it's important to set an agenda for the meeting. Some will say that it's a plan for what you want to accomplish in the meeting. I say that it's a brief statement of what you hope the client will walk away with after the meeting. Try to make your agenda mirror a benefit statement for the client and keep everything you do focused on your client's needs. In the office technology business, our agenda can look like this:

"Mike, thank you for taking your time to meet with me. From an eagle's-eye view, we specialize in understanding the way documents flow through our client's organization. We help identify any bottlenecks, if they exist, and work together with our clients to improve productivity and control and reduce all costs associated with document creation, distribution, archiving, and destruction. Most of our clients have greatly improved some of their internal processes, and some have realized savings of over 25 percent from what they were currently spending. We hope that we can do something amazing for you as well.

"Our goal today is to learn about you and see if there are ways you may benefit from a complimentary, in-depth analysis of your current workflow. Does that sound good? Is it okay if we ask you some questions to get a better understanding of where you are today and where you'd like to go?"

If you're selling one product and all your customers benefit the same way, your agenda will be much more focused and simplified. It can sound like this:

"Mike, thank you for taking your time to meet with me today. By the end of our meeting, you will have a much better idea of how you can [insert a buyer-focused benefit statement, such as *improve employee morale or increase your sales or attract better talent or improve your payroll process and free up some time*]."

It can be any statement that helps identify how they could gain something valuable by working with you. Once the agenda is set, I recommend that we always ask, "Is there anything else you'd like to cover today?"

If there is nothing else, we ask for permission to ask them a few questions. When they agree, we can proceed.

Asking the Right Questions

Though every sales opportunity is unique, the one thing they all have in common is that we must figure out the right questions to ask to uncover the true needs of the client. It's been proven that people buy emotionally and justify it logically, yet many sales professionals never attempt to ask the type of questions that evoke emotions. Why is that? I believe it's because we often confuse our need to sell a product with the customer's need to fill a void or to improve a situation. This is the main reason so many salespeople show up with brochures about their company and products, talk 90 percent of the meeting, and never uncover what the customer really needs (though they think they do). Way too often, I see a sales rep frustrated because they submitted a proposal and the customer went silent. I always ask them a few questions, which helps me learn why the deal is stuck. The first question I ask is "What problem are you solving for the customer?" I usually hear answers like "Their contract is coming up, so they have to buy something" or "They don't like their current vendor." Neither of which answers my question! The second question I ask is "What's their reason to buy now?" The answers I hear are "I'm saving them thirty dollars per month." Also, not usually a good reason for someone to buy now!

If we don't know what problem we're solving or why people need to purchase now, it's usually because we didn't ask the right questions during our initial meeting. In this section, I want to share with you the types of questions to ask so that you can uncover as much as possible during your introduction meeting. This will equip you with information that will help you build a strong relationship, understand your client on a higher level, and ultimately become their trusted business partner. What I found is that when I ask the following types of questions, our chances of success greatly increase. Here are the five types of questions I enjoy asking that help me learn, build rapport, and develop a relationship with my potential clients:

1. Curiosity questions
2. Today questions
3. Magic wand questions
4. Stop sign questions
5. Personal reward questions

Curiosity Questions

These questions help you learn more about the way your client's company operates. Remember that I'm mainly speaking about B2B sales; however, you can do the same in B2C (business to consumer).

When Julia and I were looking to hire a CPA to help us with our taxes, we were interviewing many people until someone recommended Bill Caldwell from Caldwell and Company in Bethesda, Maryland. When we sat down with Bill, he was full of energy, an expert in his field, and it was evident that he loved what he did. I've never met an accountant as vibrant as Bill prior to our meeting. Bill has been our CPA for the last six years, and I can remember exactly when we decided to select him over everyone else. When we first sat down, Bill had a very welcoming smile, looked at us, and said, "Tell me about Eric and Julia." I realize that this seems like common sense to most people, but if you've ever interviewed CPAs, it's very rare that they would ask this type of question. At least it was for us. Bill wanted to know everything! Where we grew up, how we met, our lifestyle, our goals for the future, what we enjoy doing, places we've been to and ones we'd like to travel to. He was genuinely curious about us, and that was one of the main reasons we chose Bill to be our CPA. He was very qualified and recommended, just like all the other CPAs we interviewed, but the main difference with Bill was that he made us feel comfortable and showed us that he cared about us, not just our business.

Whether you're in B2B sales or B2C sales, I'm asking you to be like Bill. Care about the people and companies you're serving and make them feel comfortable with you. Here are some examples of curiosity questions you may find helpful to use during your introduction meetings.

- I know you're extremely busy. What are all the things you're responsible for?
- What do you love about your job?
- What do you enjoy doing when you're not here?
- How many people are on your team? Do any of them report to you? Do you like that aspect of it?
- Who do you usually report to?
- What are your biggest projects over the next twelve months? Twenty-four months? What's most important? How did these projects come up?
- What's the toughest project you've had to deal with since you've been here? Why was that the toughest?

I'm sure you will come up with more curiosity questions as you think through the details you want to know about your client. By asking curiosity questions, you're able to learn a tremendous amount of valuable information about the people you're dealing with. The reason I believe this is so important is because, after is all said and done, people will buy from people, and they will make their decision based on emotions. It's going to come down to the person who made them feel like they can be a trusted partner and who cares about their clients winning! Asking curiosity questions will give you a tremendous advantage because you will have keen insight into what your clients care about and what's truly important to them on an emotional level.

Today Questions

Before we can help someone improve their current situation, it's imperative that we understand where they are today. One of the mistakes many sales reps make in this section of questions is that they begin selling. This is a big no-no! For example, you may hear the prospect say, "One of our biggest issues today is that we have physical files all over the place, and it takes a long time to find a document when we need it." Many sales professionals will stop the questioning and say something like "Well, you're going to love our solution. It is designed to help you find your documents within seconds." Or, if you're in real estate, you may hear a potential buyer say, "We want to move because our house only has three bedrooms and we've outgrown it already. We need at least four bedrooms." Some agents will pull out their portfolio of homes or open MLS to search for four-bedroom homes. I'm asking you not to do that! Our job, at this point, is to understand and *not sell*. Stay humble, listen, and take as many notes as you can, because you're going to be building a case for why they should move forward. I'll explain that in more detail in the next section when we talk about the magic wand questions. For now, just take notes and ask questions; don't try to sell anything at this point! Here are some examples of today questions you may find helpful to use during your introduction meeting.

- What's your current situation?
- What works?
- What doesn't work? Why?
- How are invoices processed today? (If you're selling invoice-processing services.)
- What do you love about your _____ (car, home, boat, company, purse, shoes ... whatever the topic is)?
- Why?
- What do you not like about_____?
- How does _____work today?
- How is this preventing you from_____?
- Who makes decisions about _____?

Today questions will give you a clear understanding of the current situation. If you listen closely, you'll be able to hear what your client loves, and you'll understand what they don't care for. It's important that we stay curious throughout the whole process and really try to learn as much as possible. Remember we're only at the introduction meeting and we have not earned the right to sell them anything at this point. Make sure that you're not making a rookie mistake of jumping into the sales pitch as soon as you hear the first pain point.

Magic Wand Questions

Recently, I found myself in a situation where it was the end of the month and I was dealing with an undecided church pastor. We had a good relationship, but he had a great relationship with a competing representative from a very reputable company. What made this even tougher was that we had access to sell the same products and similar services. Knowing what I was up against, I sent the pastor a picture via text message. It was a picture of a magic wand. I immediately followed up with a call and confirmed receipt of my text message. The pastor was laughing and was a bit confused. I asked him this question: "Pastor, if you waved a magic wand to get the most incredible deal you could for the church, what would that deal look like?" I followed up by saying, "I'm not sure that I can make it happen (because I wasn't really sure), but if I can do everything you ask for, will you move forward with me?"

The pastor said, "Eric, can I have a few hours to think about this? When do you need the answer by?" I told the pastor that he could have as much time as he needed and that my offer would be valid through the end of the month, which was four days away. Within the hour, I received the list of wishes! I was able to meet everything the pastor asked for and ultimately was awarded the church's business.

Magic wand questions are questions that help our potential clients feel like they're taking control of the situation. These questions essentially give them the opportunity to tell us what they want our solution to look like and at what price point. This is the time I ask for them to create something "ridiculous" that they won't be able to say no to. One of the many benefits for me is that I now have a clear understanding of what it would take to win their business and what they're thinking about. The beautiful thing about magic wand questions is that they allow the client to use their imagination and really paint a picture of what they want. People know exactly what they *don't* want, but very seldom do they have an idea of what they do want. Magic wand questions evoke the amazing picture of what our clients are searching for, and this is a tremendous tool for a curious sales professional like you and me. If done correctly, we'll have a clear understanding of what our client is trying to achieve, and we'll be able to better align ourselves with their vision. The sales professional who can listen and coauthor a plan to help their client reach the goal they're striving for will gain a new client.

The magic wand questions are strategically asked after today questions. It's very likely that we will uncover pain points when asking today questions. One example of a pain point from the today-questions section was "One of our biggest issues today is that we have physical files all over the place, and it takes a long time to find a document when we need it."

Remember when I said, "Don't start selling yet"? That's because it's imperative to take notes, acknowledge the issue, and save it for more questioning and to dig deeper into the actual issue. Now, during the magic wand questions, we can bring that issue up again and ask some more questions. It would look like this:

"Mr. customer, you said that one of your biggest issues today is that you have physical files all over the place and it takes a long time to find a document when you need it. If you had a magic wand that could completely fix that issue, what would your operation look like?"

This question will facilitate a great conversation and will allow your client to share with you exactly what they want the result to look like. Isn't that wonderful? That means you will now be able to align your solution with their desired result, the key word being *their*, not *our*.

Other magic wand questions are as follows:

- If you had unlimited resources and all the talent at your disposal, what would you improve? How did you come up with that?
- What would that look like?
- Why is that what you'd want?
- Can you explain what the perfect scenario would look like for you? Why?

- If we're speaking one to two years from now and everything went exactly as planned, what does _____ look like?

If you notice, I always follow up with a why type of question. This is because it's important to understand the feeling behind their desired future state. It's one thing to hear the vision, but knowing why they chose that as their desired result helps us understand the person on a much higher level. As we're going through this process, we're building a relationship. Our goal is to truly understand the other person, what makes them happy and what doesn't. Learn about their struggles and their desires. Figure out their pain points and learn their pleasure points. It's not just about selling something; it's about gaining a relationship, building trust, and helping someone achieve something they truly want.

Stop Sign Questions

Stop sign questions help us uncover the true barriers that are *perceived* to stand in people's way. Notice that I said perceived to stand in people's way. Whether the barriers are real or not, if the client perceives them to be real, it's vital for us to uncover their reasons. Therefore, it's very important to meet with the person who has authority to make decisions on behalf of the company. They're the ones who have a clear picture of their barriers and who will be able to articulate it better than anyone else. I'm not suggesting that you have this person involved in every little step of the process. As a matter of fact, that may slow everything down for you. What I'm saying is that after the introduction meeting, they may delegate the process to someone who reports to them. However, to learn as much as possible and to gain true understanding, it's always best to interview and build rapport with the final decision maker.

The stop sign questions are a wonderful tool that will help you facilitate a deeper conversation with your clients. It's by design that we ask them after the magic wand questions. They are intended to help the client think through the things they perceive to be holding them back. The answers to these questions will help you understand the true barriers and will better equip you to find ways to remove them or work with them, for your client.

Before asking a stop sign question, you may find it helpful to preface it with a statement. Usually it will be a statement of something you learned from the magic wand questions. It could sound something like this:

"John, you said that if you had a magic wand, your operation would _____." Following that statement, you can freely ask the stop sign question. Here are some examples of stop sign questions:

- What's preventing you from achieving that?
- What barriers do you have to deal with that I haven't asked you about yet?
- What's held you back from achieving_____ in the past? Do you think it will hold you back now?
- What's the biggest obstacle you must overcome to achieve _____?
- On a scale of one to ten, how important is it for you to achieve _____? How come you didn't rate it higher? What's more important nowadays?

Some of the things I discover during the stop sign questions phase give me tremendous momentum with the buyer's journey. These questions open doors that could be much harder to open if I fail to ask them. In addition, they help me build tremendous relationships because they allow the client to open up and have a deeper conversation about what they truly want and what obstacles they have in their way.

Personal Reward Questions

In my experience, people who ask personal reward questions are some of the top sales professionals in their industries. Remember people buy emotionally and justify it logically. I've emphasized this point many times, and it's so true, isn't it? Think of the last thing you purchased. Why did you buy it? My guess is that it made you feel a certain way. That's usually the case. As I'm thinking about this, I can't help but laugh at the way I recently purchased a new car. I was driving a five-year-old BMW 5 series, which I absolutely loved, and was a few months away from paying it off. I wanted to see how it felt to be without a car payment and was on a mission to pay it off. However, every time I saw a newer body style 5 series BMW, I couldn't wait to pay my car off and then go buy one! As it turned out, my car needed some repairs, which would have cost a few thousand dollars. Without any hesitation, I upgraded the car to the newer model I really wanted. The funny thing about it was the way I justified it. I said things like "Well, the payment isn't going up, and I can drive this car, which is so much nicer than the old one." I also told myself that there were no guarantees that if I fixed the old one, it wouldn't have more issues soon.

Those were all wonderful, logical justifications for my emotional decision, weren't they? We all buy the same way, and we all justify it in our heads. That's why you can help a child eat for fourteen cents per day. Helping children is emotional. Paying only fourteen cents per day is the logical justification. Spending $50,000+ on a wedding is emotional. How do we justify it? Well, it's the day we've been waiting for our whole lives. We'll only have one wedding. Sound familiar? I know because I've been there and have seen others do the same thing. And guess what? Your customers are no different! They have emotional reasons for buying things. If you can find out what those reasons are, you will be celebrating all the sales you're bringing in.

Behind every buying decision, there is some kind of personal reward that the buyer would love to achieve. Whether they want to be recognized as the person who found the best solution for a problem or they want to help other people reduce inefficient time spending and then be the hero in front of their boss, there is most certainly an emotional string attached to their buying decision. It's important to know that you can still win the sale even if you overlook recognizing personal reward desires. If your solution is a good deal for the organization and you haven't uncovered the personal reward for the buyer, they will probably still buy your product, assuming you've met all their needs. However, your chances will greatly improve if you are able to uncover the personal emotion behind their buying decision. Here are some personal reward questions that may give you the winning edge:

- If you're able to accomplish (something they said during magic wand questions), what will that mean for you personally?
- If this works, what will it mean for your career?
- What if it doesn't work? How will that affect you personally?
- What would your boss think if you could _____?
- If this happened, how would that impact your family?

I'm sure you're going to find more questions that will best help your buyer's journey as you're sitting in front of your client. Our goal as sales professionals is to uncover as much information as we can when we first meet with our client. They have problems that need to be solved and desires that they want to bring to fruition. If you're the curious person who understands those things well, you will have the best chance of differentiating yourself from everyone else who is out there only to sell their products.

Recap to Ensure Understanding

The questions all have a purpose of helping us learn as much as possible about the client and their organization, industry, vision, and goals. Once we have an understanding of these things, it's helpful to show the client that we understand them. This will help build credibility and ensure that we didn't miss something important. It's been said that the greatest problem with communication is the illusion that it occurred! Way too often, I speak with sales professionals who believe they are going to win a sale but quickly realize that the customer doesn't pick up their phone calls, doesn't answer their emails, and won't see them when they stop in. I believe the reason for this is miscommunication. The rep took notes and honestly believed they understood the client's needs when, in reality, they misunderstood the client's needs. To prevent this, I recommend that we have a recap of the conversation. This is a tremendous benefit to the buyer's journey because it

1. shows the rep was listening with the intent to understand and
2. ensures that both the buyer and the sales rep are on the same page, moving toward achieving the same goal.

Unfortunately, way too many sales professionals never recap the meeting and end up missing the mark when it comes time to make a recommendation. Please don't make this mistake; it frustrates the client and wastes their time. Once you're done with the questioning portion, feel free to say, "I believe I understand your challenges. To make sure that we're on the same page, do you mind if I recap what you said?" They will be grateful for it and will give you a few more minutes to make sure you didn't miss something important.

Coauthor a Plan

Not much could be better than to leave the introduction meeting with a concrete plan, or at the very least, scheduling next steps. You are the leader in the buyer's journey, and it's your responsibility to create the vision and next steps for the journey. Unfortunately, many salespeople hesitate to take the lead. They believe the customer will tell them what they want and how. In reality, if the customer knew what they needed and how to accomplish their desired objectives, they wouldn't need us. They have Google and the rest of the internet to gather information and buy the things they need. The reason they need us is because they're not the expert in the field; we are. They're looking for you to take them by the hand and let them know that you understand what they want and you know exactly how to help them achieve it. In essence, you want them to feel like you have their back and are fully capable of being their guide.

To successfully coauthor anything, you will need agreement from both parties. The way I've seen it work best is if the sales professional brings forth a plan and asks the client if that sounds good. It's as simple as that. The plan could be something as simple as saying, "Jim, based on everything we've discussed today, I believe that we can help you achieve (name a few things you learned from your conversation). To conduct a complete analysis for you, we're going to need to examine your (whatever you need to be successful—for example, invoices, current contracts, volumes, and an onsite walk-through). Does that sound good?" If the conversation went the way we thought it did, they will most likely agree to it. Once you have agreement, ask for the contact information of everyone who will help gather the information you need and ask for the client to make an introduction for you before you go. In the case stated above, I would also schedule a walk-through prior to leaving.

Analysis

There were many times when I was discussing an opportunity with one of my sales reps and saw them focusing on saving their potential client money to earn their business. If it's possible to do that, great. However, many sales reps make that their main objective and therefore don't often provide the best solution because they feel like they'll lose if they're more expensive. What I'd like to remind you is that no company ever goes into business to save money. They all want to add value to others by providing a great product or service to the marketplace, and they want to be profitable doing it. If we as sales professionals understand how our clients make money, and we align our product or service to help them increase their revenues, they will be happy to pay us more than what they're spending today. It will be a tremendous value-add to them and a true investment in their growth.

One of the best things you can do for your sales career is to always schedule next steps before leaving and then automatically send a calendar invite to lock it in. If you have only one takeaway from this book, please let that be it!

Follow-Up

I was recently invited to attend a meeting with one of my sales representatives, Mo. She was absolutely amazing during the meeting. She asked incredible questions and set a great agenda for the buyer's journey. What impressed me even more was her follow-up email to the client. For confidentiality purposes, I will be using fake names and times from Mo's email to the client.

Hi, Sam:

It was a pleasure to see you Wednesday—I'm sure each and every time I do will be the same.

When we see you (yes with breakfast) on *Friday, September 8 at 9:00 a.m.* (calendar invite to follow), we will be mapping this location with all the print devices (desktops) and obtaining configuration sheets from each one. This is where having a *map or fire escape diagram* is extremely helpful so that the locations for the devices are accurate. We leave nothing open for guessing—rather, our assessment is data driven for accuracy.

We also thank you for being frank with respect to the office politics, and we can assure you that we experience this often and we are extremely good at getting information from those individuals that house that knowledge without ruffling the feathers too much. You were going to speak with Lisa to obtain some pain points she is experiencing in her overworked IT role, so we can make sure we handle her challenges thoroughly.

In summation, this is what we know so far:

- There is currently no budget for upgrading/refreshing your printer fleet (this can leave you vulnerable for hardware and virus intrusion and security breaches).
- Printers are not rotated within the company.
- Your copier leases with ABC Company expire somewhere close to the end of 20xx.
- Your service contract with your ABC Company charges you more if you exceed the allotted amount each month/quarter.
- You currently are scanning, storing, and retaining the paper files offsite with XYZ Company for the mandated time you are required to by law.
- We are unsure as to where the electronic versions are stored, but Lisa would be more knowledgeable on this subject.

- Approval processes need to be tightened up (logistics, etc.).
- No software to really analyze and control costs.
- Security is a very big issue—reduce risk of intrusion.
- In your wish list of duties, you are trying to structure a purchasing system to catch errors and duplications.

I'd also like to schedule a follow-up meeting on *Thursday, September 20 at noon* where our software specialist Stan Wilson can come and ask the pertinent questions about internal workflow processes. This is an extremely important piece, as this allows us to incorporate solutions with your company that directly impact the amount of print on paper. *Someone in Finance or AP like Julie would be able to provide a wealth of information on how paper flows through your organization and should be present for this meeting.* I'll send a calendar invite for this as well just to get it on the calendar with my IT specialist and so that Julie has a heads-up.

Thanks, Sam—have a great weekend. As always, please don't hesitate to contact me for anything.

—Mo

Mo did an amazing job following up with Sam. She included all the essentials that make a follow-up wonderful. It's important to follow up with an email or a written letter (or sometimes both).

A good follow-up should

- thank the person for the time they're committing to you,
- include bullet points of your discussion and the goals you're striving to achieve,
- include a list of all the information they're supposed to gather for the analysis, and
- include a date for the next scheduled meeting or walk-through.

This will help you stay top of mind while you're guiding the client through the buyer's journey.

Conclusion

We never have a second chance to make a first impression. It's important to look at the introduction meeting as our first impression with a potential client. We must constantly remind ourselves to make it all about the client, to stay curious, ask engaging questions, and most of all, to get over ourselves and practice the wonderful principles of GOY.

Your clients will open up more if you ask the five types of questions to engage them in a meaningful discussion. Here they are once again for your reference:

1. Curiosity questions
2. Today questions
3. Magic wand questions
4. Stop sign questions
5. Personal reward questions

I encourage you to bookmark this chapter and review it prior to your initial meetings. The best part about rereading something isn't that the text has changed; it's that you've changed since the last time you read it. Every time you reread something, it's possible that you will see something you missed every other time.

If you're reading a book like this one, you're already a rock star. I'm saying that because I admire people who want to improve their skills or perhaps learn a new skill. If you don't currently have a process for your introduction meeting, or if your process is not moving your sales cycle to the next steps, I'm asking that you try the steps I've outlined in this chapter. People are always looking for a leader to guide them, and I encourage you to see yourself as that leader, especially during the introduction meeting.

Exercise: Tips for Success

As most sales professionals, you've had success, and some of your initial meetings moved to the next stage of the buyer's journey. On the other side of that are probably some missed opportunities that did not move forward. Why do you think that is? The person met with you, so it's safe to assume that they were interested in at least learning about new things or exploring your products or services. Here are some questions you can answer to help improve the customer experience during your initial meeting.

- What was different between the meetings that moved to the next step and ones that didn't?
- What do you wish you would have said or asked in the meetings that didn't move forward?
- What three things do you want to learn about the person you're meeting with (personal and professional)?
- What are some things the prospect can gain by working with you? List them out and learn that list by heart.
- Create at least three questions you can ask in each of the five types of questions:
    - » Curiosity questions
    - » Today questions
    - » Magic wand questions
    - » Stop sign questions
    - » Personal reward questions

Practice your questions until they come naturally to you.

CHAPTER 8
Proof It!

You can see a lot by just looking.
-Yogi Berra

Now that your team has completed the analysis, it's time to schedule a proof of concept meeting with your client. There are two parts to the proof of concept: the internal meeting prior to meeting with your client and the proof of concept with your client. The proof of concept is your opportunity to find out exactly what the client wants and—just as importantly—does not want from your recommended solution. At this stage of the buyer's journey, our goal is to show them a solution that we believe will help them achieve what they want and receive feedback on how we may be able to tweak it to best meet their needs. Remember—you're the expert, and the client may not necessarily know what's best for them until they see your idea in action. In the car-selling world, this is the test drive. In real estate sales, this is the open house. In retail clothing stores, this is where the customer tries on the clothes. This is the proof of concept, or in another term, a demonstration of our product or service.

Our goal is to introduce a concept that we believe will work for them, show it to them, and welcome feedback and criticism of our solution. At the end of the day, the only opinion that is going to matter will be the client's. The proof of concept meeting can be held in their office or yours. If you have a product that you're able to showcase, it's better to show it at your location. The reason for that is because it places you in a better position to control your environment, and it's easier to have the resources readily available at your office in case something goes wrong. It also shows how serious the client is about working with you. If they refuse to visit and simply ask you for a proposal, it's not a good sign.

Prior to the proof of concept meeting, it's imperative to have an internal meeting with your team. The internal meeting will ensure that everyone is on the same page and understands the client's needs. It will allow your internal team to discuss the opportunity at hand and will better equip you for the proof of concept with your client. These are the presales and postsales support people who have been involved in this opportunity, conducting the analysis and gathering data, and they may have ideas about what the best solution might be. If you're already working in a sales role, this concept might be new to your organization. Not everyone plans in such a thorough way, and many times the salesperson will just handle the whole thing. The problem with that is that the salesperson (you) may be overlooking something. Think of it this way: if you had six people sitting in a circle and someone placed one of those colorful, inflatable beach balls in the middle, is it fair to say that everyone will see different colors even though they're all looking at the same ball? I've tried it with a group of people, and that's exactly what happened. I saw yellow, green, and red, while my counterpart saw purple, orange, and blue. I think you get the ball example. Looking at a sales opportunity works in a similar way. When multiple people look at the same thing, everyone approaches it from their own unique view, with their personal idea for a solution. Some will be great, and others will not. However, you will end up with way more ideas and options to choose from than you could ever think of on your own. This type of teamwork will greatly help you achieve a winning edge!

It's unfortunate, but many salespeople are reluctant to team sell in the way I'm describing. They believe their solution is the best one, and therefore they move forward with presenting to the client without any feedback. Many times, that strategy will work; however, they may be missing a big opportunity when they do that. There is an old African proverb that says, "If you want to go fast, go alone. If you want to go far, go together." I'm asking you to team sell because I want you to go far!

Once everyone is in the room, I recommend that you answer the following three questions:

1. Why is the client interested in seeing this product or solution?

This question is designed to ensure that everyone understands the current challenge the client is trying to improve or a problem they want to solve. If there's a mismatch with your team's answers, you'll have to talk through it until everyone comes to an agreement on the problem you're solving. If an agreement can't be reached, I suggest that the lead person schedules another meeting with the customer to better understand what the customer believes they want to solve. You may be thinking, *Yeah right, I'm not calling the customer.* I would probably think the same thing! However, it's much better to admit a mistake and make a joke out of it than get further along only to realize you didn't understand what the client was trying to achieve. My experience has shown that people don't expect us to be perfect and will relate to us more when they see that we're not. There is a good saying my mentor and an amazing speaker trainer, Roddy Galbraith, always says, "They'll like you for your successes, but they'll love you for your failures." Though Roddy speaks about this when he's training speakers, I believe the same rules apply for sales professionals. I believe that our failures and mistakes will help us better connect to our audience and customers on a deeper level.

If everyone agrees on what the client is seeking to achieve and why, feel free to move to the next question.

2. How is our solution going to improve their situation?

This question gives the team an opportunity to hear what the client is going to hear once the solution is presented to them. It's vital to verbalize what we're trying to accomplish. Just like in the beach ball example, when someone articulates how the solution will improve the client's situation, all other team members will be able to hear it and visualize it from their own points of view. This may provide an opportunity for questions that had not been thought of before and additional collaboration to ensure a no-brainer for the client.

3. What are we missing?

This is a wonderful opportunity to reflect on all the conversations your team had with the client. It may be useful to compare notes and make sure that every one of the client's desires is covered. By asking, "What are we missing?" you're able to rely on one another to see the things you may have overlooked. I cannot remember a single time when a rep asked me this question and we weren't able to find something that was missed. In addition, I often rely on

Vince, the president of DCA Imaging Systems, to help me answer that same question. I realize that Vince's thought process is completely different from mine. As a matter of fact, nine out of ten times, we see things differently, and he always has a unique perspective that opens my mind to new possibilities. I absolutely love having access to Vince and his thought process. Every time I consult with Vince, I know there is a great possibility I will gain another option or see something I wasn't able to see before. In the end, the people who benefit most will be our clients or my sales team. I encourage you to assume that you're missing something and try to find it with a team. It will pay tremendous dividends in your sales and leadership career.

If you and your team are certain that you've thoroughly answered the three questions above and you can clearly articulate the solution in terms of why the client will benefit, it's time to schedule the proof of concept meeting.

To ensure this meeting is most effective, I recommend creating an agenda for your meeting. This will guarantee that you and your client are on the same page. What follows is an example of an agenda that I would follow. Feel free to use it if you find it helpful!

Meeting Agenda

Since it's beneficial to focus on our client more than ourselves, I always recommend asking three questions in the beginning of the proof of concept meeting. These questions will help you stay aligned with what your client truly wants and what they believe they need. The first question I ask is this:

"Has anything changed since we last spoke?"

It's good to be up to date with your client's status. If you're not, you may be opening yourself to some unpleasant surprises. I've actually had people tell me that they decided to take another position and will be leaving the company within a few weeks. It's important to know stuff like that! On the flip side, I've had some clients answer enthusiastically and tell me that they're so excited to see our solution because what they have going on currently is upsetting everyone. It's good to know things like this as well.

The second question I ask is this:

"What are you hoping to accomplish today?"

I follow up by saying that we know what we want to show and have a great agenda lined up. I add, "I just want to make sure that we cover all of your expectations and answer all of your questions while you're here." This shows that we're prepared and that they are very important to us.

The third question I ask is this:

"What are you most excited to see today?"

This is a pleasure question. Even though we're programmed to find and fix pain points, I've learned from Jeffrey Gitomer that finding pleasure points is much more effective. By understanding what they're excited about, we will be able to gear our proof of concept toward the things they are looking forward to achieving.

Review

During the review portion of the proof of concept meeting, we have an incredible opportunity to show our client that we truly did listen, and it will once again ensure that we're on the same page. This is your chance to shine! As I mentioned earlier, it's been said that the problem with communication is the idea that it occurred. Many people feel like they haven't been heard, and many people only listen to respond instead of to understand or learn.

This is the part where you recap the following:

- what happened when you met the client
- what they said their challenge is
- what you spoke about before

Ask, "Is there anything else that I may have missed?"

Many salespeople fall into the trap of "knowing" what the customer needs without ever checking to see if anything has changed or if the client is still on the same page as they are. This causes miscommunication and ultimately the client going dark and not returning phone calls. If you want to stand out and really wow your client, continue to always ask questions and ensure you're in alignment with their needs.

Objectives

Once you complete your review with the client and you're on the same page with them, it's good to share your objectives for the proof of concept with them. I recommend that you have your objectives established prior to your meeting; however, it's always good to leave room for their input in case you missed something. The objectives should come from all the information you've gathered from your client, team, and analysis. These are the things that you will help improve or eliminate from their environment.

For example, the client is not able to find invoices that were paid in a timely manner, and I want to present a software that will allow them to find any invoice within a matter of seconds. My objective would be: "*Demonstrate how you will be able to quickly access your invoices.*"

You may have several objectives, and that's fantastic. Feel free to list them in a row. Once you've gone through your objectives for this meeting, make sure you leave space for that one question, "Is there anything else you'd like to see today?" If they say yes, write it on your easel, digital board, or paper and have a blank box next to each objective. Once you've accomplished each one, you can ask if they're satisfied with what you showed them. If their answer is yes, feel free to check off what you've covered, or have them check it off. It can be fun!

Before They Go

I share my home office with my wife, Julia. We actually have matching desks across from one another, so we sit with our backs to each other, facing different walls. Oftentimes, after we put the kids to sleep, we go into the office to finish up work or plan something new for the family. This particular evening, I was reading something, and it motivated me to ask Julia a simple question I'd never asked her before. I turned to her and said, "Honey, how can I be a better husband?" Little did I know, Julia has been working on that list for years and had it readily available, as if she had been waiting for me to ask that question for a long time! I'm slightly kidding about her being ready with a list, but she did share a few things with me, which told me exactly what I needed to do to be a better husband in her eyes, the only eyes that matter! I didn't argue and did not attempt to defend myself; that would just be silly. I simply became more aware of her needs and made the changes she was asking for. The amazing thing is that if I hadn't asked, she would never have told me, and I wouldn't have been able to improve and be more of what she wanted. The other part of it was that she was extremely touched by the question. I received tremendous kudos for even caring about what she thought. I must have been really lousy at showing her that her opinions matter to me prior to that night, which was another thing I started to improve on.

I believe the same strategy will work for you with your clients, if you simply ask the right questions. Once your proof of concept demonstration is complete, it's a good idea to sit down at a table to ask them for their honest feedback and opinions. They'll appreciate it. Here are some good questions to ask:

- What did you like the most?
- Did anything surprise you?
- How do you see your organization using our solution?
- What would you improve about the things we presented today?
- What would you like to see in our proposal?

You may notice that you're actually getting closer with your client during this step. That's because you showed them that you care about improving their situation more than you care about making a sale. When I say, "You showed them," I'm hoping that you authentically feel this way. It's no good to fake it and act like you're trying to help when you're only going for the sale. I'm asking you to go after the relationship harder than you go after closing the deal. Why? Because when sales reps go after closing the deal, they pay more attention to how they can make more money instead of how they can best benefit the client's needs. I've seen this happen over and over, and I assure you that it never comes off as authentic, and your clients will see right through it. Here is your chance to be better than anyone else they're dealing with. Show them that you care, and they will begin to know you, like you, and trust you. Help them solve their challenges while always ensuring they're the most valuable in this relationship, and they will stay with you for a long time.

Before you say goodbye, make sure to schedule the next step of their buyer's journey, the validation meeting or the proposal meeting. The reason I gave you two options is because you have the choice of either combining the validation meeting with the proof of concept demonstration or scheduling it separately after the proof of concept. For the purpose of this book, I'm going to write as if we scheduled it separately.

Tell Me What You Want to Buy

The proof of concept is my second-favorite step in the buyer's journey. The first? Winning the deal of course! I really enjoy the proof of concept because that's where we build the relationship and coauthor the solution with our client. Therefore, it's so important to have a plan in place and to meet with your team prior to the client's visit. Here are some great questions to answer in your planning meeting:

- Why would the client be interested in the solution we're going to propose?
- How will our solution improve their situation?

- Why is that important to them?
- What are we missing?

During the proof of concept, our goal is to show them what we believe will be the best solution for their organization. By using the steps outlined in the chapter, we keep the communication open and allow the client to share their ideas, concerns, and thoughts about our solution. When done correctly, the client ends up telling us exactly what they want to buy.

After your proof of concept meeting with the client, it's important to sit down and ask them the following questions to make sure that you understand where their mind is and what they're thinking.

- What did you like the most?
- Did anything surprise you?
- How do you see your organization using our solution?
- What would you improve about the things we presented today?
- What would you like to see in our proposal?

Before they leave, make sure that you schedule the next steps in the buyer's journey.

CHAPTER 9
The Waitress Technique

Coming together is a beginning, staying together
is progress, and working together is success.
-Henry Ford

The validation meeting is an opportunity for us, the sales professionals, to listen to what our client wants to buy from us. This is a time when we collaborate, listen, and tweak our solution to give them exactly what they want. The best part? It greatly increases our chances of earning a client and building a stronger relationship. During the validation meeting, we provide the client with a detailed proposal, without any pricing. We discuss our conversation during the proof of concept meeting and share with them what they wanted to see. Then we ask them if anything is missing or if our solution is exactly what they were looking for. Based on their answer, we'll be able to move toward the proposal or further tweak our solution.

When I lose a deal, I always like to receive feedback from my clients to make sure I understand why they decided to go with my competitors. This practice also helps me learn from my mistakes and grow as a sales professional. It would be a shame to make the same mistake more than once. I remember a specific instance when I lost a deal and went to the client to get a better understanding of why they made their decision the way they did. I was positive that I did everything I could possibly do to win their business and was prepared to hear that I lost it because my recommendation was more expensive. The client gladly met with me and told me that the reason I wasn't awarded the contract was because my solution did not meet some of their needs. I was shocked. My team completed the analysis and demonstrated the technology, and I was confident that we had covered all their needs. She told me that she sent me an updated email after our demonstration, which explained their additional needs, but I did not receive that email. When she went into her sent folder, we realized that she misspelled my name. What a bummer that was.

Later that week, I was dining at a restaurant and noticed something that had happened thousands of times before, but it was never as clear to me as it was this time. After the waitress took everyone's order, she addressed each person at the table again and repeated what everyone wanted one last time before sending the order to the kitchen. She validated what we had just ordered to make sure she hadn't missed anything and to give us a second chance in case we changed our minds. She also asked, "Is there anything else I can get you?"

That's when I realized that if I had done what this waitress did and taken my time to reiterate the solution prior to submitting my proposal, I would have greatly increased my chances of winning. That simple validation of the solution would have allowed me another opportunity to make sure that what I was selling would meet all their needs, and we would have uncovered the fact that I missed an important email! Many B2B sales professionals go from initial meeting to proposal without much in between, and they end up losing more deals than they win. I'm asking you to incorporate the validation meeting into your buyer's journey. It will help you tremendously.

Conducting the Validation Meeting

The validation meeting can occur as a separate meeting or combined with the demonstration, while the solution is fresh on our client's mind. To speed things up, it's easier to have it combined with the demonstration meeting, especially if the solution is fairly simple. However, when the solution is more complex, I prefer the validation meeting as a standalone meeting. It gives the client time to digest what they experienced during the demonstration and discuss their findings with their internal teams. It helps generate a more productive conversation when we meet to validate their solution.

The validation meeting is all about coauthoring the solution with your client. I recommend starting off by asking if anything has changed since the demonstration meeting or since you've last met. If things have changed, listen intuitively and find out why the change occurred. If nothing changed, it's good to proceed with sharing what you designed as the solution. It really is just like the proposal meeting, which we'll discuss in the next chapter, but you have a chance to make changes, and you do not discuss pricing at this point. Once you've presented your solution, ask questions to learn everything you can about

- what they think of your solution,
- what they would like you to change about your solution,
- how it could impact their organization,
- what that impact would mean to them on a personal level, and
- anything that would prevent them from moving forward.

By focusing on these areas, you will uncover some things that you may not have been aware of before. In addition, they're observing you and your competition throughout this process. If you do this in a consultative manner, with their best interest in mind, they will see that you truly care about providing the right solution, while your competition already proposed pricing and is now hounding the client every day to see when they'll be making their decision. Allow the competition to make you look great.

If you have one takeaway from this chapter, please let it be this: if your client makes changes to your proposed solution, your next step is another validation meeting. No matter what, do not present pricing until your client agrees on the solution you're going to be presenting to them. If there are changes, it's a good chance that they may have missed more things and will need to change something else. Make sure that you go through the whole validation meeting the same way the second time as you did the first time. Try not to assume that you know anything and pretend as if it's the first time validating the solution. It's the safest way to go. If the client likes what you're recommending and has no proposed changes, then you can move forward with scheduling your proposal meeting.

I believe that the validation meeting is the most important meeting throughout the buyer's journey and encourage you to begin implementing it within your sales process if you don't currently do it.

Tips for the Validation Meeting

Validation is the easiest thing we can do to improve our chances of winning the sale. Think about all the times you've been left wondering what the client thinks after presenting the proposal to them. Some salespeople fall into the trap of submitting the proposal only to call and leave voice messages without receiving a call back. If you've experienced that in the past, I highly suggest adding the validation meeting to your repertoire.

Here are some good questions to ask during the validation meeting:

- What do you think of our solution?
- Is there anything you would like us to change about our recommendation?
- How do you see this impacting your organization if everything worked exactly the way you envision it?
- If it does what we say it will, will you be the hero?
- Is there anything that would prevent you from moving forward?

If they have changes to your recommendation, tell them that you'll take care of it and schedule another validation meeting to make sure that everything is in order prior to proposing your price. If they agree with everything you recommended, be sure to schedule the proposal meeting prior to leaving.

CHAPTER 10
The 6 Elements of a Winning Proposal

Try to leave out the bit readers tend to skip.
-Elmore Leonard

I remember one of my sales reps coming into my office with a beautifully bound proposal. The cover looked professionally done, and it was spiral bound, had tabs for different sections within his proposal, and even had charts and maps that would fold out to show a bigger picture of his illustrations. I could tell that he spent a lot of time on this proposal, and he was extremely proud of the way it looked. When we sat down, I asked him to walk me through it the way he would do it for his potential client. He was so excited and passionate about this proposal that I wanted to see how amazing his presentation would be, and he wanted to show me. He was ready.

As he began, he started speaking about our company history and where we started out. He spoke to me about our leadership team and all the wonderful experience each of the leaders had. He then continued to share a list of clients who currently did business with us. Once that was finished, he spoke of the manufacturers that we represent, in this case it was Xerox, their history, financial standing, and even their other divisions. We then came to a page titled "Proposed Equipment." He went on about every piece of equipment he was recommending and the features that he believed they liked. That was followed by a page titled "Proposed Costs" and had a list of pricings broken down with options for various lease terms and purchase options.

Once he was done with his presentation, I asked him two questions:

1. What problem are you solving?
2. Why would they buy from you?

As you can imagine, the response I received to my why question was all about our company, Xerox, the financial history, and so on. When I pressed a little further about what problem we were solving, he simply didn't know. Though his proposal looked good on the outside, it was filled with information that was not important to the client. Unfortunately, he was not awarded that contract. I wasn't involved with that client and therefore didn't know what other mistakes were made on our behalf throughout this buyer's journey. If I had to guess, just by listening to the proposals, we missed many steps along the way, including understanding the client, their needs, their bottlenecks, their setbacks, and problems they'd like to solve and building a relationship, to name a few.

Sales is hard. However, like my friend John Maxwell says, "Everything worthwhile is uphill." I believe that sales is the best possible profession in the world, and it takes hard work to be successful. Many people believe that just because they like people and can speak to anyone, they're going to be great at sales. Unfortunately, nothing can be further from the truth. Sales is more about listening and understanding than it is about speaking and making yourself look good. It's never about the seller and is always about the buyer.

Our proposal should be a statement that says, "We heard you loud and clear, Mr/s. customer. We understand that you're facing these challenges, we are aligned with helping you meet your goals for this project, and we have a way to get you what you want, in the most efficient way possible." If your proposals already portray this message, then I applaud you. If not, you may find some good tips in the pages to come.

In the following section, I want to equip you with tools to help you build a proposal that will not only answer all your client's questions but also help you look more attractive to them.

Writing Your Proposal

The goal of the final proposal should be to paint a picture. This picture should show where the client is today, what they hope to accomplish and why, how will our solution help them achieve their goals, and the type of investment it will take for them to reach their desired state. In the simplest form, I recommend that your proposal includes the following sections:

- executive summary
- current scenario
- goals and objectives
- proposed solution
- financial overview or proposed investment
- about us

Sometimes our proposals require additional sections. That's completely fine. What I'm hoping you'll take away from this chapter is that each proposal should be created specifically for this client. Many sales professionals like to take old proposals and modify them just by changing some figures and the name of the solution. I get it; it saves time, and you don't have to do that much work. However, I challenge you to be careful about where you try to save time. It took you tons of effort, cold-calling, relationship building, analyzing, presenting, planning, and stressing just to get to this point of the process. Instead of saving time here, I suggest you turn on the turbo boosters and place every bit of energy into your proposal. Make it specific to your client. Show them that you listened. Express that you understand their organizational needs and that you have customized a solution that will help them go where they desire to go! The reason I'm so adamant about your proposal is because I know that most great sales professionals are not strong when it comes to writing proposals. Let's face it. These are two completely different skill sets.

If you're not capable of creating a proposal that reflects all the things I described above, perhaps you can work with one of your sales administrators to help you create what you're looking for. If you don't have a sales administrator or anyone within the company who can help you, you can pay someone to create it for you. It will be a small price to pay. If you meet all the criteria and present a professional document that helps you win the business, it will have been well worth it, right? The other thing it may teach you is that sales is like running your own business. It will feel entrepreneurial to hire someone for your proposal writing, and once you've experienced that, you will be on a whole new level the next time you meet with a business owner.

Now, let's break down each section of the proposal to gain a better understanding of the purpose they will serve in helping you win more business.

Executive Summary

The executive summary should be no more than two pages (one if possible) and is designed to summarize your entire proposal. The reason for having an executive summary is in case there are people who will be involved in the decision-making process who were not involved in any meetings until this point. These people could be owners, C-level executives, or someone who's in a different department and location altogether. Our goal with the executive summary is to give those people an overview of what our proposal entails.

A good executive summary template is usually broken down in the following way:

Paragraph 1
Thank you for giving (your company name) the opportunity to present a solution for (whatever issue they want to solve or improve).

Paragraph 2
Currently you're experiencing (give a summary of what they're going through or current scenario).

Paragraph 3
By partnering with (your company name), you will be able to reach your goals of (list their goals) and attain your desired outcome (paint a picture of what their improvement will be once your solution is implemented).

Paragraph 4
We are the best partner to help you attain your goals because (list a few reasons why you're the best company to partner with).

Paragraph 5
We're completely committed to your success and achieving your objectives. Thank you for the opportunity …

The key to a good executive summary is to focus on summarizing your proposal in a way that it's all about them. We want to eliminate fluff as much as possible, and even if you're working for Apple, don't boast about how amazing your company is! This is not the time, and if you start talking about your company, you begin to make it about you, not them!

Current Scenario

The current scenario section is designed to illustrate the way things are working now. Unfortunately, many salespeople believe that their main goal throughout the sales process is to learn about the customer's current spending. I've seen mistakes made when the salesperson writes only about current expenses in the current scenario section. The challenge is that the salesperson is starting to make it all about price without the client necessarily asking for it. When that occurs, the only logical thing that happens from there is that the salesperson tries to show their price to be lower than the client's current spending to win the deal. I'm asking you not to corner yourself like that. Many people are willing to pay extra for something more valuable to allow them to increase their revenues. I suggest that we refrain from showing any current expenses at this stage of the proposal. Instead, describe the operation as it is today. It may also be a good idea to add some of the limitations the organization is experiencing due to the way things operate presently.

Feel free to format it any way you'd like. I prefer bullet points and small sentences to make it easier to read, but you can certainly find something that works best for you. Once again, consider the possibility that your proposal will be handed to someone who has no knowledge of your work with the company. Your goal is to make it detailed enough for them to understand what's going on yet simple enough for them to get through it quickly.

Goals and Objectives

The goals and objectives section is a place where we want to list out all the things the client is looking to solve. Some of the objectives could be to

- create an atmosphere of joy at work,
- improve middle-level leadership,
- improve invoice processing,
- increase sales,
- pay invoices faster,
- onboard people efficiently, or
- reduce shipping expenses.

Each client will have their own unique goals and objectives. It's your job to figure them out as you're building your relationship. The main point is that we want to ensure our proposal is in complete alignment with our client's goals and objectives. If we get to the proposal stage and we don't know the client's objectives, it's safe to assume that we are presenting a proposal a bit too early. I recommend slowing it down, getting back in front of the customer, and asking a few more questions. After all, we don't get paid for delivering proposals; we get paid for solving problems.

Proposed Solution

Not too long ago, I was approached by Vince, the president of DCA Imaging Systems. He was pretty upset. He showed me a one-page proposal he found on one of our office printers; it was evident that a sales rep forgot to grab it after printing it. This proposal had a picture of the device in the center of the page and a statement that read, "Proposed Solution." The president was dumbfounded. He showed it to me and asked, "Eric, how can we say this is a solution? What problem are we solving with this proposal?" I knew exactly what he meant; the proposal did not identify the client's challenges or their goals.

The proposed solution is designed to describe in detail how partnering with you and your company will help your client achieve their goals and objectives. It's supposed to show your client how you're going to solve the challenges they're facing and why your services and products are the absolute best solution for them. The most important part of this section is that it focuses on the solution.

As people, we tend to think in pictures. I'll give you an example: When you hear the words "A fox had a white tip on its tail," do you, like most people, visualize the white tip? Or do you see the words "white tip" spelled out in your mind? Knowing that people think in pictures, we're able to paint a beautiful picture of their desired outcome in this section of our proposal. I challenge you to minimize saying things about your actual product, service, or solution, and maximize describing the end result in their organization. In other words, you can say something like "Once [name of your solution] is implemented, your organization will experience [vividly describe a desired end result that your client was striving for]."

Financial Overview or Proposed Investment

There are two schools of thought as to where to place the financial overview (pricing) page. Many sales trainers and gurus will tell you to always leave the pricing as the last page. I can see how that makes sense. Oftentimes, though, I've placed the financial overview right after my executive summary. I think you'll know when to do what. I did that when I knew that my solution came with cost savings. This takes the edge off the client and allows us to have a wonderful conversation about their objectives and how we're going to meet them. Typically, they're more relaxed to have that conversation when they know that, no matter what, my solution will be a cost reduction for them.

When the solution calls for our client to increase their expenses, even though the value-add is there and they will truly receive way more services or products for their money, I recommend having the financial overview page toward the end of the proposal. This gives us, the sales professionals, time to walk the client through our amazing solution, paint the picture, and get their agreement about how much better their life will be after they partner with us.

Once the pricing is presented, I always ask them, "What do you think?" Then I stay quiet until they answer. You may hear things like "We have to think about this" or "I'll present it to the board" or other types of answers that don't give much information. When this happens, I ask them specifically, "Did you think my price would be higher or lower than it is?" Based on that, we start a conversation. Our goal is to never leave the proposal meeting feeling unsure of how the client felt about our proposal. We want to make sure that we know exactly where we stand with them, especially when it comes to finances.

About Us

By the time they're reviewing your proposal, if you've done everything we've discussed doing during the buyer's journey (up to this point), they already know everything they need to know about you and your company to allow them to make an intelligent decision. The purpose of having the "about us" section is if they have to present your proposal to someone who has not met you or your company yet.

While many people believe this should be the first section of the proposal, I like placing the "about us" marketing piece in the last section. It takes a lot of maturity to step out of the way and realize that people are not doing business with us because of all the things we're capable of, our history, and our accomplishments. They're doing business with us because of the specific things we can help them with.

Make it all about the customer and always place their needs ahead of telling them about you. One of the best ways to do that is to place the "about us" section in the back. The "about us" section will most likely be a document that your company already has on file. It describes things like the company's history, why they do what they do, their experience, and why they're the best choice for the client's products and services. This should be the only place in your proposal where you talk solely about your organization.

Conclusion

If you've ever listened to John Maxwell speak or have read any of his books, you've probably noticed that he keeps his delivery very simple. Someone once complimented him on having that gift and asked how he's able to simply describe any topic. He responded, "I just like to put the cookies on the bottom shelf, where everyone can reach them."

I'm asking you to put the cookies on the bottom shelf and try not to impress people with big words and complex statements. Keep your proposal straight to the point. I always ask myself, "Would I be able to explain this proposal to my seven-year-old son, Max?" If not, it may be too complicated. I'm not saying that you should write your proposal in crayons. The point is we should try to keep our proposal as easy to read as possible and allow everyone an opportunity to understand its contents. No need to impress people with highly technical terms if there is a way to say it in laymen's terms.

If you follow the steps outlined in this chapter, I'm confident that you will increase your chance of winning the business. Wishing you the best of luck with your proposal writing and impressing your clients by making it all about them!

Exercise: Tips for Success

If your buyer's journey is like the one I've outlined for you in this book, I'm pretty sure your customer knows if you're someone they would like to award their business to, prior to you ever submitting your proposal. However, even though the proposal may not help you much, it can definitely hurt you if done in a lazy way. Let your proposal make you a star in front of the people who will be evaluating it, though they haven't met you yet. If your proposal is professional, looks good, addresses all their needs, and lays out a good plan for your client, your contact will be your internal champion all the way.

Please make sure you have a similar layout that addresses the following sections. If you don't have a good template for your proposal, feel free to use this as your guide:

- executive summary
- current scenario
- goals and objectives
- proposed solution
- financial overview or proposed investment
- about us

CHAPTER 11
Answer with a Question to Close the Deal

There is only one way to get anybody to do
anything. And that is by making the
other person want to do it.
-Dale Carnegie

W hen I first started out in sales, I was just as excited about giving someone a proposal as I was closing some sales. Back then, I didn't close many sales; I was still learning. Being young and optimistic, like most salespeople are, it's easy to get excited about giving someone a proposal. Deep down inside, there is something that tells us, "We definitely got this deal" and it feels so real! I remember having eight to ten proposals out to different customers and hopelessly waiting for someone to call me with the good news. Unfortunately, those calls rarely came. I understand now that I did not have an identified buyer's journey back then and was not experienced enough to schedule next steps before ending a meeting with my potential clients. It's easy to walk away excited, thinking that all the customer needs to do is get approval and we'll get the deal.

This is where most sales professionals get surprised. They start calling the customer to follow up on their proposal and have no luck with getting to the customer. It's like they fell off the face of the earth, isn't it? Have you been there? I have, and it sucks! They stop replying to emails, don't respond to voice mail, and if we stop by, they seem to always be in a meeting. So how do we prevent it?

Follow-Up

The best thing we can do to follow up with our client is schedule next steps before leaving the proposal meeting or any other meeting for that matter. To be successful in this game of sales, we always—and I mean *always*—have to schedule next steps with the client before ending the meeting. Once the proposal is presented, it is our job to have the client explain their internal process of how they're going to be making their decision. Then we can ask them to schedule the next step in the process. It's easy for the client to say, "As soon as we know something, we'll contact you." That's an easy copout. If you've conducted your analysis and built the relationship the way we've discussed in this book, you should understand their timeline, and at some point, they would have shared a desired implementation or change date with you. If you're working a deal now and you don't have a good understanding of the client's desired date for implementation, I suggest you ask them. This will be the date that everyone is working toward from the beginning of the project. If there is no desired date to make a change, how serious is the client about your solution?

If you covered all the bases and everything is going perfectly, most likely your follow-up is scheduled and you're in complete control of the next steps. That's exactly where you want to be. A good practice for when someone tells you they're going to follow up with you is to ask them, "If I don't hear from you by a certain date, when would you like me to call you?" There will be many times when the client says they'll call you on a certain day and never do. In those cases, feel free to follow up with them on the date you both agreed to. Make sure you follow up when you say you will.

If you're in a situation where your client is nonresponsive, and you were not able to schedule the next steps, it can become uncomfortable to follow up. I mean, how long do you call and send emails, right? The worst is calling for the tenth time and actually getting the person on the phone, isn't it? What do you say then? "Um, hi, just calling to check in on the proposal I gave you?" No way! If you somehow got yourself in this position, try to examine how that happened and avoid doing the same thing in the future. For the time being, I recommend getting creative with your follow-up. The way that works best for me has been to always have a new reason for my follow-up. It must be more than "I'm just checking on my proposal." After all, if they had any update for you, they would have called you by now. There is absolutely no need to call them three times each day to see if anything has changed.

I remember one of my previous companies implemented the Rep of the Month award for their salespeople. By winning the award, the rep would have their picture on a wall, with the month they won the award, and a nice parking space. Their picture was seen by everyone who walked into the company, including their clients. As soon as they implemented that award, I won the rep of the month title seven or eight months in a row, until I parted ways with that company. It was something I was proud of achieving. One of the months, I was coming in a close second place, and to make it more painful, the person who was beating me was my mentee. I was happy for him and very proud that someone I was mentoring was having a great month, but deep down inside, I did not want him to beat me. Would you? I'd be the laughing stock of the company! Or so I thought. There we were on the last day of the month, and I was running out of options. I decided to contact one of my clients; I had provided them a proposal, but they were in no rush to make it happen this particular month. I called my client and was told that he was going to be in meetings all day. Go figure! I asked them to call him out of the meeting and to tell him this was an emergency. I was pretty resilient back then, and most of all, I did not want to break my rep of the month winning streak. When my client came to the phone, I told him that if he signed the contracts today, I was going to give him a tremendous incentive. When he asked why I was in such a rush, I told him the truth about being in jeopardy of losing my rep of the month streak, and he was more than happy to help. Not to mention he was getting an amazing deal for doing this. I drove over to his office, and his receptionist handed me the signed contract with a smile. He waved at me from his meeting behind the glass door, and a huge sigh of relief took over my body.

I learned a few valuable lessons from that experience. First lesson was that our clients want to help us win if we've established a good relationship with them and always strive to help them win. The second lesson was that there is an incentive to help everyone decide faster. When you're stuck and the client has gone dark, what do you do? Can you offer a special incentive to help move the sale along, or do you just call and ask if they have a decision made?

Following up is an art because you have to walk that thin line between persistent and annoying. When a proposal is delayed, I like to redirect and take the client out to lunch or dinner. Once we're one-on-one, it's easier to get to know each other on a personal level. I've learned that people really do open up to us when we open up to them. My goal is to always be authentic and genuinely curious. I want to learn about their family, goals, ambitions, and hobbies—not just talk about work and the status of my proposal.

If you don't have anything new to present, no incentives, and no lunch or dinner, your follow-up will most likely not get you much further. Take your time and think about your client. What would get them to move? If you don't know, ask them. I have no problems asking my clients how we can make this deal happen within a certain time frame. If it's possible, they let me know, and if it's not possible, they also let me know. Once you know what incentive can make them move faster, you can reach out to them with a specific request or opportunity to help them expedite their decision any time you need to close a deal.

I wish I could tell you a rule for how often to follow up, whether to stop in or call, to send a letter or email. Unfortunately, that doesn't exist. There is no specific talk track, and every client will react better to a different type of follow-up. You should know your client well enough to understand what type of follow-up will work best with them. If you don't know, ask them directly. The best thing we can do as reps is prevent the whole thing and schedule the next steps before leaving the proposal meeting. Even if the client says, "I need to think about it." Smile and ask, "How much time will you need?" Once they tell you, schedule a meeting for that day on both of your calendars, while you're in front of the client. Prevention is the best way to go in this situation.

Closing

When we talk about closing the deal, we mean getting agreement from the client that they're going to buy our product and service and signing contracts. It's that feeling of accomplishment, pride, and relief. It feels like what a team would look like after winning the national championship!

For some reason, everyone puts closing ability on a pedestal. We see the famous quote "coffee is for closers" on T-shirts, posters, and coffee mugs. The ABC method of selling stands for Always Be Closing. It's funny how much pressure salespeople place on themselves to be known as closers. The challenge with focusing on closing a deal is that we can miss all the important steps that cause us to close it in the first place. See, closing a sale is not where the success is. This is simply where you're recognized for your success with this customer. The client probably knows who they're going to do business with way before the proposal is ever presented. To close well, we must begin the process well and continue to wow the customer every step of the way.

So why am I taking the time to write about closing? Because this is the meeting where many salespeople leave money on the table. We get so excited about the possibility of getting a signed contract that we give away free stuff or promise things that weren't previously agreed to. I'm as guilty of this as anyone else. Our emotions take over, and the thought of us not getting a signature, when we thought we would, overrides our logic, which causes us to make irrational and unnecessary decisions just to make a deal happen.

When we come to a closing meeting, we should have all the paperwork filled out as much as possible. If this happens to be a surprise and you have an opportunity to close a deal faster than expected, your experience will be slightly different. This is when your client may want to negotiate. What works best for me is to always answer a question with a question. This isn't a sales tactic or being sneaky. I seriously want to understand why the customer is asking the question. For example:

Client: Is this the best price you have?
Me: What price were you expecting to pay for a solution like mine?

Client: How quickly could you deliver?
Me: When do you need it by? Why?

Client: Does this include a license for my admin team?
Me: Did you need a license for the admin team to be included? Why?

I can go on all day with these examples, but I think you get the point. Let's understand why they're asking the question, and then we can move forward. If a question comes up that you're not sure how to respond to, feel free to ask, "Why do you ask?" This will open a dialogue and will help you understand what your client is thinking about. Oftentimes, the real question is behind the one they asked you.

I've seen way too many sales professionals overspeak when they absolutely don't need to. They try to overvalidate their solution at the closing table, after the customer already told them that they want to buy. If you are given the signal that you won the deal, that's the time we stop selling. There is absolutely no reason to say anything else about your product or service unless specifically asked a question. Why am I saying this? Because we may say something that the customer did not think of, which could prolong or change their decision. It's much better to just get the contracts signed without giving them any further reassurance that they made a great decision or that your solution is amazing. After all, they already came to that conclusion!

When coming to the closing table, it's good to sit on the same side as your client, or across from them if there is no table between you. When we sit on the same side of the table, we all get the same perspective. Now we're partners, working to solve the same issues, for the same company. It's not us versus them; it's just us! Once you try this technique, you'll see exactly what I'm talking about. I try to use this in every situation when I'm communicating with another person. When there are no boundaries between two people and they're both looking in the same direction, with the greatest intentions for one another, only the best can occur. The only thing left to do at this point is get the contracts signed.

Congratulations on closing your deal! Now, it's time to overdeliver and really start building that relationship with your client. It all begins after a sale is made!

Tips for Following Up

Following up is a tricky skill to possess. You have to be good enough so that the client is receptive—yet not too needy that they may get turned off. The best thing to do is always have a full pipeline of other things you can be working on. When you stay busy with other accounts, it is easier for you to come off as a true professional and not seem needy. If it's been way too long and you need to follow up, try getting creative with it. Make the interaction fun, exciting, and unexpected. What are some creative ways that you can follow up with people after presenting your proposal?

- Invite them to a dinner or a sports event.
- Stop in with doughnuts for the entire office.
- Create an unexpected incentive (work with your sales leader on being creative).
- Email them an interesting article.
- Send them a lead.

I'm sure you can come up with a few more things to help you stand out and have an effective follow-up. All you have to do is think about it and ask your teammates for suggestions.

When you're at the closing table, remember to answer their questions with a question. You want to understand why they're asking prior to giving them an answer. Congratulations on closing the deal!

Part 3

They Picked Us! Now What?

CHAPTER 12
The T-Mobile Failure

Good judgment comes from experience, and
experience comes from bad judgment.
-Rita Mae Brown

Postsales is the marriage after the client says, "I do," and signs your contract. It's not very common that two people date for years, get married, and the night after the wedding, one leaves and stops calling for a long time. Unfortunately, if we look at a sales relationship between a salesperson and their client the same way we look at a marriage, the salesperson often disappears after the contracts are signed (the wedding night). In this chapter, I'm going to show you ways to strengthen your relationship with your client after they buy from you. It will allow you an opportunity to sell them more products and services and to become a true partner for them.

As a young sales rep, I received a territory with no current accounts. This meant that I had to hunt. Since I didn't know anything else, I just learned to hunt well and never complained. My job and income depended on getting new business in the door, and that's exactly what I did. When I closed a new account, I didn't spend too much time with them postsale. I just simply moved to finding the next opportunity. Within a year of being in sales, the top rep on my team resigned, and I was assigned her territory. This was a whole new world for me. This territory actually came with a pretty nice base of existing customers that the previous rep had cultivated through the years. Without being in the "farming" mind-set, I simply attended to the customers who had an opportunity to upgrade their technology right away and ignored the ones who had recently purchased something from our company. Remember I was a hunter. I would close a sale and move to find the next opportunity.

After a year in the new territory, I began to notice that some of my current clients were leaving my company for our competitors. When I met with them after getting the bad news, many of them had the same story. They told me that it was because they didn't have a relationship with anyone in the company. I came to a quick realization that "anyone" was me and that I had failed at building and maintaining relationships with the company's current clients. I did not do a good enough job taking care of my customers. As a matter of fact, I ignored them, and my competitors swooped in and built a relationship while I was out looking for new customers.

I learned a valuable lesson back then, and I hope to share that lesson with you. Many sales professionals believe that it's all over once the sale is made. The lesson I learned was that the closing of a sale is the beginning of a new chapter, not the end. I can relate the same to an expecting mother! When my wife was pregnant, I remember thinking how nice it would be once the pregnancy was over. Boy was I wrong! The birth of our first child, Max, was just the beginning. The same applies for the sale and gaining a new customer.

Once they're on board and have decided to partner with us, the real nurturing should begin. We should treat them as delicately as a newborn child. Care for them, love them, serve them, and help them grow. That's the best way to build a relationship and a true partnership. Don't do what I did and neglect your customers. Please learn from my mistakes!

Postsale Implementation

Today, we have a good process to ensure the postsale implementation goes smoothly. A good process would typically consist of the following:

- a meeting between the client and your implementation team to coauthor a plan for delivery of the goods with minimal disruption to the client's operations
- internal meeting between everyone who has a role in the implementation process to ensure your team completely understands the client's expectations and that each individual understands their role in the process
- an amazing implementation of your products and services

The postsale implementation is your company's chance to make a great first impression. This is where your client finds out that they made the right decision, or they start to regret their decision of doing business with you. The postsale implementation is extremely important, and I highly recommend that we treat it as if our whole deal depended on it.

To make it work well, I suggest you schedule two meetings: an external implementation meeting with your client and an internal implementation meeting with your own team.

External Implementation Meeting

This is the meeting where you, your team, the client, and their team coauthor a smooth implementation of your products or services. You will discuss things like delivery and which floor to start with. Identify the stakeholders and their responsibilities and ensure that everyone has your contact information so that all inquiries, requests, and modifications can go through you and be communicated well to the rest of the team.

As the sales professional, you're the quarterback of the whole process. Do not give that responsibility to anyone else, because they will never care about your customer as much as you do. Take full responsibility for all the good, bad, and ugly, and you will always come out on top. It's a good idea to invite the presales and postsales teams to this meeting. I like doing this because it allows all of us to understand the client's expectations, and our team becomes better aligned to deliver exactly what we promised during our sales process. The teams ask the client technical questions, and the client prepares the team for things they may not have thought of.

After winning a large deal, we went through the implementation process with every possible stakeholder. We scheduled the delivery and implementation teams and had IT services ready to connect everything in order to minimize downtime for our client. We had thought of everything and felt like it was perfectly scheduled. When we got there first thing in the morning, as agreed to by all parties involved, the CIO of the customer's company pulled me off to the side and said, "I think this is going to be too much of a disturbance. Let's begin the implementation and roll out after 5:00 p.m. when all our people go home." What was I to do? This meant that we had to hold the trucks and a whole bunch of people overtime, which we did not anticipate and had not agreed to. As the leader of this project, I had to decide quickly. You know, the customer is not always right, but they are always the customer! How could I empower the CIO and make this a win-win for everyone? At this point, my team was pretty frustrated because the plans were being switched last minute, so I had to calm them down first. Then I asked to meet with the CIO. The best thing I could come up with was to pull out the implementation schedule that everyone had agreed to, and I went over it with him. I then told him that we would be more than happy to accommodate; however, it would come at a greater cost to the company, which I knew he wasn't authorized to approve. I then reassured him that we had this implementation planned to the most basic detail and that we would not be a disturbance to anyone, if he allowed us to continue as we initially discussed. He quickly gave me the green light, and we moved forward with a flawless implementation.

If we had not had the implementation meeting with the client, I would have had nothing to go on. It would have cost us and the client way more time and money than anyone anticipated, and our first impression would have been a dud! In this case, the implementation meeting saved us and allowed us to stick to a plan that everyone had agreed to.

Internal Implementation Meeting

Prior to delivering the goods, I suggest holding an internal implementation meeting as well. I recommend inviting everyone who has something to do with the implementation process. I like having someone from logistics, operations, IT, presales support, postsales support, and admin joining the meeting. I do this because I want everyone who's going to be a part of the process involved on the front end to ask their questions and raise concerns about things that I may not have thought of. By giving them the floor to be a part of the process and encouraging them to ask questions, the whole team will be better equipped to flawlessly deliver what we promised. The other benefit is that they feel like they matter. We know how incredibly valuable our support teams are to our sales process. By giving them an opportunity to be heard, they, in turn, feel like an important part of our sales process, which always helps build a better team atmosphere.

If we do all the necessary things to ensure a smooth delivery and implementation, we will wow our client. Unfortunately, way too many salespeople rely on others to make the implementation go well. Their belief is that once they close the deal and bring in signed paperwork, their job is done. I know this because it used to be my belief. The company probably agrees that sales should hand everything over and step out of the way. If your company feels this way and you have to follow their process, that's perfectly fine. However, I still recommend that you, as the sales professional, stay on top of the people who are taking over and ensure that there is proper communication between your team and the client. Remember: just as no one will ever care as much about your child as you do, no one will ever care as much about your client as you should. Take responsibility for their satisfaction, and you will be rewarded by referrals and continual business. Give that responsibility to someone else, and they may ruin your relationship without you ever knowing.

Reviews and Check-Ins

Once everything is in working order, how can we continue to add value to our client? Some of the ways are ongoing account reviews, pop-ins, and the one that's worked best, referrals to help them grow their business.

Account Reviews

These reviews can be held on a quarterly basis, but sometimes the client prefers to do them semiannually. Every now and then, I may get a request to conduct them once per year, and I usually convince the client to hold them more frequently.

Why are the reviews so important?

- Reviews allow us to be proactive about supporting the client's ever-changing needs.
- They keep the lines of communication open.
- They give us knowledge about news within the account.

- They keep us in front of the decision makers.
- They help validate our value within the account.

I remember sitting in a review with one of our clients, a prominent university in Washington, DC. As usual, we started off with small talk to catch up, and then we moved into the formal account review. During the first part of our review, we discussed what our team had done since the last review, showed kudos our team had received from the university's staff, shared any problems that had been solved, and discussed issues that were still ongoing. We also updated the client on any training our staff had received to support them better and provided them a snapshot of how they were using what we sold them.

During the second part, we asked all about them. As soon as we asked the first question, we knew that everything was going to change moving forward. Our first question was "What's new?" The client looked up and said, "Well, I'm going to be retiring at the end of this year." At that moment, we realized that our relationship with that university could be in jeopardy. We had a great relationship with this client, who was the ultimate decision maker for our contract. Unfortunately, she kept our relationship close to her.

The good news was that we found out early. This gave us time to stay on top of the transition and offer all the help to her we possibly could. As she was training her replacement, guess who was there? That's right. We were. We helped the incoming person understand our solution (which was a multimillion-dollar-per-year contract that no one wanted to lose) and most of all get comfortable with our team and the support we provided.

If it hadn't been for that account review, we could have been surprised by our client's retirement and would have missed the opportunity to meet and build the relationship with the incoming person.

There have been many other instances where we asked the question "What's new?" during the account review, and the client opened up about new initiatives and projects they were going to be working on. Many of them were able to use our products and services, which we never hesitated to offer at that time.

By knowing what's going on within our accounts and always being able to help them achieve their goals, we become an unreplaceable asset to our client. If you're currently not preforming account reviews, I encourage you to start conducting them. Show the client what your team does for them, learn about how you can support them better, and then support them the way they want to be supported. Don't ever let them leave for a competitor because they didn't think you were valuable enough to their organization.

Pop-Ins

When we're prospecting for new business, pop-ins can be pretty annoying. So I call them strategic stop-bys! That's because we're strategically stopping by with more information, and our goal is to move the sales process along. However, once the organization becomes your client, it's great to just pop in. I like to randomly stop in with pastries or lunch for the team and just talk to them about how everything is going. This stop-in does not have to involve the decision maker at all. It's simply checking in with the end users to make sure everything is going well and hearing from them if there are any issues that may be lying dormant. In addition, the pop-in helps to build a rapport and relationship with more people throughout the organization, which will help us serve the account better and result in keeping them as a client for much longer.

Referrals

When people hear the word *referrals*, they automatically think of ways they can get referrals from their clients. I'm actually speaking about giving referrals to your clients. When was the last time you gave a referral to your client? If you haven't, why not? If I have a client who specializes in moving businesses and I meet with a company who's going to be moving, I feel like it's my duty to mention my client who moves organizations. This way, I can be helpful to the new company I'm meeting with, and most of all, I help my moving client grow their business. One thing I've noticed is that once you give your client a referral, they never forget about it. When I do it, I don't want anything in return; I just want to be a value-add for my clients.

Are you thinking about your clients when you meet a new organization? When we refer our clients and help them grow their business, we show them that we're more than just a vendor. We show them that we're a true partner who holds their best interests in mind. We show them that we don't just come around when there is a potential deal on the table for us and that we really think about their well-being even when we have nothing to gain from it. This is where we become a true partner. So, who do you know that your clients can help? It may be a good idea to create a list and then send an introduction email (if they agree) to connect the two parties. I assure you that your client will always remember your efforts to help them grow their business.

Conclusion

One of my longtime customers was a small church who bought one copier from me back when I first started out. I remember their copier having issues on a Friday, the day they were printing their Sunday bulletins, and my contact called me up in a panic. She said, "Eric, your technician just left, and he did not have the parts to fix our copier. He said he has to order it and that he'll be back on Monday to fix it. What am I going to do about my bulletins?" At this point, I knew that if she sent them to a print shop, my company would reimburse the church, and they wouldn't be out of any money. However, I wanted to show her that she was special to me and that I value our relationship. I asked her to email me her file. I stayed late that evening and printed the five hundred bulletins in our showroom, in color (they only had a black-and-white copier at their church), and delivered it to her within a few hours. After praising the Lord for a while, she gave me a huge hug and told me that I was her lifesaver.

The following Monday, she gave me a call and said that the head pastor wanted to meet with me. When I showed up to the meeting, the pastor thanked me and told me that they'd never had this much positive feedback about their church bulletins. The best part was that he wanted me to upgrade their older copier for a brand-new device with color capabilities. It's amazing how going out of the way to help someone can pay off. I guess Zig Ziglar was right when he said, "You can have everything you want in life, as long as you help others get what they want."

It happens way too often that salespeople neglect their clients after the sale is made. Sometimes it seems like they care more about new business than they do about their existing clients. What a shame. I often see this with cell phone companies, and it always baffles me. Why is it that a new customer gets special rates and discounts to switch over from their current carrier, but the current clients, who may have been with this company for years, aren't eligible for the same special promotions? That's just silly! I know they have to keep their margins up to please the shareholders, but at some point, they should really make sure that their current clients are being appreciated as well.

If you want to establish a strong, long-lasting relationship with your client, make sure you follow the steps outlined in this chapter. Start the relationship strong by holding implementation meetings to provide the best transition for your client. Conduct account reviews two to four times per year to really understand where your client is heading and their initiatives for the future. Suggest ways you can be a better partner for them. If you're in the area, pop in to say hello. Perhaps some doughnuts or lunch for the office from time to time would place you in a great position to expand your relationship within your client's office. Refer your client's company to other clients and friends so that they can grow their business. Remember—when they grow, you have a better chance to benefit as well.

I hope you're convinced that we build our relationship after the sale is made. If you don't currently have a plan in place, perhaps a few pop-ins this week could prove to be beneficial for you. I'm wishing you the best of luck in building your relationships with your existing clients. If you haven't done so yet, right now is the perfect time to begin!

Build Rapport after the Sale

Building relationships with our clients pays off phenomenal dividends. Are there clients of yours who have not seen you in a while? Perhaps you can do something special for them this week. Here are a few suggestions to help you build a relationship with your existing clients:

- Write a thank-you and appreciation email or letter out of the blue.
- Pop in with cupcakes for the office.
- Send them a lead for their services.
- Offer to volunteer time and help them with community service or outreach (if applicable).
- Take your contact out to lunch or dinner and learn about what's going on with them.
- Schedule a quarterly review with them to go over their account in detail. Learn about any initiatives on their horizon.
- Ask them if there is anyone you can introduce them to, since you're always networking, and make the intro if you can.
- Call to see how everything is going, without needing anything.

What's the one thing you can do this week to build a closer relationship with a few of your clients? Building relationships requires being intentional about wanting to build relationships. It's not something that just happens. I suggest that you take one or two of the bullet points above and schedule them for a customer in your calendar. Treat it as if it's the most important meeting of your week and see how much it pays off for you in the not-so-distant future.

CHAPTER 13
The Magneto Effect

Work harder on yourself than
you do on your job.
-Jim Rohn

No matter what company you go to, what business you start, or what client you attempt to attract, you're always going to take you with you. Why not take the best you possible? Do you have a plan for improving yourself to attract the type of clients you want? In this chapter, I'm going to give you a few ways that you can become better known as the expert in your field. Our goal is to have people think about calling you when they think of the product or services that you sell.

In the last few years, I became obsessed with personal development. I've invested in courses, seminars, and life coaches to help me become better in many aspects of my life. In fact, the best investment we can ever make is in ourselves. One of my favorite teachers is the late Jim Rohn, who said, "Work harder on yourself than you do on your job." This statement really resonated with me. As I began to focus on improving my skill levels in leadership, communication, sales, public speaking, coaching, thinking, and writing, I noticed my life taking a turn for the best. I improved my relationship with my wife, my children, my coworkers, my friends, and my family. I became more attractive to potential buyers who began to not only hire me for leadership training programs and life coaching but also offer me positions within their organizations. I believe the best compliment we can ever receive from our clients is a job offer after they bought something from us. It truly shows that they were impressed by what we did for them and want us to be a part of their organization. The reason I'm talking about this is because I realize how much our lives can improve if we become a subject matter expert within our business. If you've read this book until this point, then it's safe to say you're serious about your career and improving your sales skills. I'm asking you to take it one step further.

Learning how to sell is great, but learning why people buy is much better. Learning closing skills is wonderful, but having people come to you because you're the best there is will serve you more. You see, I'm saying that so you can start thinking differently. Start attracting clients to you instead of always trying to hunt for new business and convincing clients that you're the best.

Whether Apple is the best company for phones or not is not for me to discuss. We all have our own opinions about which brand is the best. However, every time they have a new iPhone launch, people are sleeping in front of their stores all night just to buy it. Has Apple ever called you to try to sell you their phone? Most likely not. Why is that? Because they built a loyal following.

Maybe we'll never have people sleeping outside of our company to buy our brand-new product, but we can certainly begin to create a name for ourselves as the expert in our field. To accomplish that requires about an hour of your time each day. Yep, only one hour! And it will pay huge dividends if done correctly. Can you find an hour to help take your income to a whole new level? I bet you can.

Here are a few things you can do to become a value-add to the marketplace and begin attracting clients.

Learn

Learn as much as possible about the industry you're in. As a sales professional, your clients are looking to you for guidance. They want you to understand your industry so well that you're able to help them make a buying decision that will not only be good for them today but serve them well into the future. How well do you know your competition and their products? If you don't know them well, why not? Everything is available online, and Google can be your best friend. Knowing about where your industry is headed, what your competition is offering, where you're positioned the strongest, and what type of benefits your products and services bring to the marketplace will give you a tremendous advantage with your clients. So let me ask you, When is the last time you learned something new about your industry? What's the one thing you can learn about this week to help you be better than you are right now?

As a new rep, I got my foot in the door with a very large company and started to build a relationship with many people in their office. Within a year of building rapport within this company, they decided to send a bid out for their copiers and printers. This was going to be my largest deal yet, and I was excited about the opportunity. It definitely helped my confidence to know that their team knew me better than they knew their current sales rep. At that time, I didn't know much about my industry and really had no clue about any competitive products. I knew my product line extremely well and was convinced that I was selling the best technology out there. By the way, if you don't feel that way about what you're selling, and your numbers aren't where they should be, it could be because you're lacking confidence in your product or service and may need a job change to sell something you're more passionate about. Back to my story. The client had a graphic need that the competition did better, but at that time, I did not know that about my competition. Remember I was convinced that I was selling the best product in the industry. Through my passion and relationship, I won the biggest contract of my life (at that time). Unfortunately, I parted ways with the company I worked for prior to the implementation of the solution I sold to this client, so I was not there to see how things went.

About one year later, I bumped into my contact from that company at a deli during lunchtime, and I asked him how everything was going. He was quick to express his frustration. He told me that some of the things I sold him did not meet his needs the way I was convinced they would, and the company, overall, was not taking care of them like I promised they would. I was very embarrassed after our conversation. It made me feel bad to know that I had sold something that simply wasn't true, even though I was sure it was. From that day forward, I made it an obsession to learn as much as I could about everything that involved my industry, my client's business, the products or services I sold, and the ones I competed against.

I never want to be the smartest guy in the room; no one likes them. However, there have been many times when my knowledge of the industry or technology helped the client make a more intelligent decision. I love hearing, "Thank you for bringing that up. No other vendor told us about this." The best part about being a subject matter expert is that people are confident to refer you to their friends and clients, which will pay off tremendously in the long run.

Write

Now that you're learning, let others know what you know. It's so easy to write an article on LinkedIn or post something on Facebook and Twitter where thousands of people will be able to see your content. You can even target the people you want to see it. When I began to learn leadership principles and got certified as a leadership trainer, I started a blog. You can see some of my writing at www.thegoalguide.com/blog-updates to get an example of what I'm talking about. I started to write about attracting people, becoming a better leader, improving communication skills, and of course being better in sales. Every week, I would post my article on every social media outlet that would allow me to post. Before I knew it, people were reaching out to me to come speak to their leaders, to train their teams, and to speak at their meetings. I didn't have to make a single cold call for this to happen. I simply put helpful content into the marketplace, and people found it valuable enough to reach out to me.

The important takeaway here is *value*. I've learned to never confuse what I want to say with what people may need to hear. When I write, I always think of my audience and how I can best add value to them. So, if you're in the jewelry-selling business, perhaps an article on how to shop for jewelry is a good idea. If you're in health care, writing about new regulations and how they can affect doctors and patients in the future could be beneficial for your potential clients. No matter what business you're in, there is a market of people who are interested in learning about how they can optimize their organizations by using your products or services. Help them learn!

Once you write something, feel free to email the article to a potential client and to your current client list. They may find value in it. Also, find out from the people you meet what they're interested in learning about; learn it first and share it with them. It's simple to become a value-add, but it takes hard work and discipline to pull it off.

If you're not a writer, you can always learn to be better. When you first begin to write, you're most likely not going to see results right away. It's going to take some time to see positive results. However, if you stay consistent and write something weekly or monthly, people will begin to react. They will post comments, ask questions, and begin to invite you in to learn more about your area of expertise and how you may be able to help them. This is one way of knowing if your writing is effective.

If writing is absolutely not your thing, don't waste time getting good at it; it's not for everyone. In this case, you can find articles that were written by others and share them with people who you think will benefit the most. All they'll remember is that you were the expert who sent them the article, regardless of who wrote it.

Speak

I believe that public speaking is the most valuable skill for a person to possess. Think about how we vote for politicians. It's usually the person who connected with us the most, and it's usually through their speech. Fortunately for us, many people fear public speaking way more than they fear death. Pretty wild, right? This means there aren't many public speaking experts in your field, and you can become the one people gravitate to ... unless you'd rather die than speak in public! If you're like I used to be, and you get extremely nervous when it's time to speak in front of a crowd of people, just know that you can become better at speaking, and there are ways to get rid of the anxiety. The number-one way is to do it more often. That's right—conquer your fear and speak as much as possible. You may also find it beneficial to join a Toastmasters group. Just Google it in your area, and you'll be amazed at how many of them exist close to you. You can also take courses on how to become a better public speaker. Just like most other things, speaking is a skill that we can improve on. A few years ago, when I had to speak in front of people, my heart would start racing, my stomach would turn, sweat would pour, and anxiety would take over. Today, I'm completely comfortable speaking in front of any crowd, and it's all due to training, practicing, and speaking more often.

When I was selling record-retention and document-management services, one of my teammates, James, was an expert at record retention. He was asked to speak by one of our clients at a conference for law firms. After delivering his speech on best practices for records retention within a law firm, he added tremendous value to the attendees. The best part was that he showcased himself as the subject matter expert in front of hundreds of people. Within days of the conference, we received a call from a national law firm. The woman stated that she had heard James speak at this event, and she wanted us to consult her on their firm's record-retention policy. We would have missed that opportunity if it hadn't been for James's speech.

I realize that what I'm asking you to do may be outside of your comfort zone, but that's exactly where growth happens. At some point in your career, you had to make a first cold call. Do you remember how uncomfortable that was? Who can ever forget? I bet within a month you were walking into businesses, ignoring the No Soliciting signs, and speaking with people as if you owned the place! The same will happen with everything that you try and stick with until you succeed. One lesson that always helps me is remembering that anything worth doing is worth doing poorly. Your first speech isn't going to be good, but that's okay! Your second one will be much better. Your first article will most likely not get any views, and that's okay. The second one will do much better. What I'm constantly learning is that if I don't write the first article or give the first speech, there is a 100 percent chance that I will never write the second article or give my second speech.

If you want to experience results you've never had before, you must do things you've never done before. There is absolutely no way to do what you've always done and achieve results better than you've ever achieved. What we achieve is in direct proportion to what we do on the front end. So I'm asking you to stop doing what everyone else is doing; stop following the (m)asses because sometimes the m is silent. Instead, get creative with attracting your clients. If you learn, write, and speak, you will connect on a much higher level, and you will be the one your clients are seeking instead of the other way around.

Tips for Becoming an Expert

When people think of your product or service, do they automatically think of you as the expert in that field? What do you know that others can benefit from? Here are some things you can do right away to get your name out there and start attracting people to you instead of always going after them.

- Post helpful information on social media
  - » three programs to help nonprofits acquire technology
  - » five tips so you don't get burned when buying a house
  - » what you must know before signing your mortgage agreement
  - » three best practices to sell your home quickly
  - » best way to avoid a cyberattack
  - » ten questions to ask when interviewing a candidate

- Vlog—record yourself speaking about one of the things above that applies to you and post it on social media.

- Attend conferences and ask to be a speaker on one of your topics.

- Ask your clients to conduct a "lunch and learn" (L&L). This is where you or the client provides lunch and you educate them on ways to be more efficient or best practices in your field of expertise. For example, if you sell IT services, a good topic for an L&L could be "how to prevent hackers from getting your information."

Doing these things may not be difficult for you, but they will require your time. The best way to find the time is to schedule it. Wake up even earlier, stay up a little later, write during lunch, record "five-minute tips of the trade" when the idea comes to you throughout the day and post it on social media. I bet you'll notice an influx in interest about your products or services. You must get creative enough to stand out from the crowd if you want to achieve greater results. Good luck!

CHAPTER 14
Final Thoughts

It's not what happens to you but how you
react to it that matters.
-Epictetus

In my mind, there is absolutely no better career than sales. When the economy is down, many companies begin to downsize but usually look for ways to boost their sales. Though they downsize, they don't get rid of people who produce revenues. When the economy is up, we need salespeople to fulfill market demands. Buyers will always need a good salesperson to take them on a buyer's journey—to help them uncover their true needs and acquire the products and services that will help them achieve their goals. While good salespeople are becoming harder to find, the demand for them keeps growing, and every company is looking to hire a good salesperson.

In this book, I shared the principles that have been modified, tested, remodified, and tested some more throughout a decade. These principles work best for me and the salespeople whose success I'm responsible for.

In part 1 of this book, we discussed preparation for the sales game. I spoke about having a clear vision, an optimal morning routine, and creating a plan for the week. So let me ask you—what's your vision? What does your morning routine consist of? Do you have a clear plan in place for the week you're in right now?

If you're not sure about how to answer these questions, what steps can you take right away to help you improve what you're currently doing?

In part 2 of this book, I shared the importance of a buyer's journey with you. The journey that I like to take our clients on is as follows:

- introduction meeting
- analysis
- proof of concept
- validation meeting
- proposal
- follow-up
- closing

- implementation
- relationship building and future sales

Have you taken the time to identify a great buyer's journey for your ideal client? Think of the client you're most proud of having won over. Why did that client come to mind? My guess is because you worked hard for it, outmaneuvered the competition, and won the business. Is that a fair assumption? How can you do it all over again? What steps did you take to win that client over?

You see—sales is a process that can be replicated over and over. The key is to reflect on the deals you win and duplicate all the things that went well. Then reflect on the deals that you didn't win, understand why, and try to avoid making the same mistakes again, if they are mistakes that you can control. Of course, "The competition was half your price" is not something that you can control; however, you can help the client see why the competition is half your price and why your solution is a better value, if it actually is.

Final Thoughts

In sales, you're going to experience setbacks, rejections, and surprises, and you're going to deal with dishonest clients from time to time. Things are going to happen that are completely out of the blue, and they will make you want to scream and cry at times. It's important to understand that even though you may not be able to control what happens, you are in complete control of how you handle it. I'll share a recent experience with you.

I woke up one morning with excruciating back pain. I usually follow the old marine corps belief that "pain is a weakness leaving your body," but this pain was not going anywhere. It was so bad that I decided to swallow my pride and go to the emergency room to get checked out. After the x-rays were done, the doctor sat down with me and said, "Eric, your back looks fine. But your heart seems to be bigger than normal. You're in good shape, so I wouldn't worry about it too much, but go to the cardiology unit, just in case." Not thinking anything of it, I went to see a cardiologist. After months of various tests and blood work, I received a call from the cardio team, and they told me that I needed to schedule a meeting with the chief of cardiac surgery, Dr. Trachiotis. A few days later, Julia and I sat in Dr. T's office as he began to explain that I was going to need open-heart surgery. When I asked what would happen if I decided not to have the surgery, he said, "The results of not doing it would be total heart failure."

That was heavy news for a healthy thirty-six-year-old male. The problem hadn't been caused by any health or diet mistakes; it was something I was born with. One of my veins ended up going from my lungs to the wrong side of my heart, which caused the heart to be overworked and overstressed. In addition, my body was not receiving all the oxygenated blood that I should have been receiving. So we scheduled the surgery for two weeks out and went home with many thoughts going through our minds.

Today is exactly two weeks since my surgery, and I'm happy to report that everything went extremely well. I made a record recovery and was walking the day after surgery. I maintained a positive mind-set throughout the process, and as a result, I feel like the luckiest guy in the world because this heart issue was uncovered. I'm grateful that I'll get to live a longer life than I would have had they never uncovered my birth defect.

We all experience setbacks in our lives, especially in the sales field. There are going to be times when you think you won a deal and you're going to find out that you lost. There will be times where you go weeks without someone agreeing to see you. You're going to face rejection and defeat, and you will, at times, feel like a failure. Just like my unexpected heart surgery, you will receive unpleasant surprises that will make you want to quit and go do something with fewer risks, fewer rejections, and less pain. I know this to be true because it's happened to me. I also see it happening to many others from my positions as a life coach and as a director of sales.

If it happens to you, know that you're not alone. It's probably a safe bet that there are a few other people on your team having thoughts similar to yours.

Know that it's completely normal and that you can work through it to get back on track to achieve all the things you want to achieve.

One way to get over the slumps quickly is to acquire the mind-set of a sales winner. Adopt the mentality of "If it is to be, it's up to me!" That's the approach that keeps the best of the best on top and separates the successful sales professionals from the ones who are not getting the results they want. Many sales reps sit around and wait for their manager to get them more training, resources, or skills. They believe that if the company had a better website, they would be more successful at selling. They think that if they had a different territory, everything would be better. The problem with that type of thinking is that it forces you to rely on someone else to help you succeed. I want you to run away from that type of thought process and instead ask yourself, "What can I do to improve my situation?" Remind yourself, "If it's to be, it's up to me!"

Here are a few things you can do to take control of your destiny, improve your success levels, and get back on track to become the top producer in your company. Someone is going to get that title—why not you?

- If you're experiencing rejection, you can take responsibility into your own hands. You can ask your sales manager, or your top sales rep, to role-play with you or to listen to you while you make calls. They will quickly be able to help you adjust your talk track.

- If you're not able to move your sales process forward after the first appointment, start bringing people with you to help you improve your first appointment skills. Ask other successful people on your team if you can join them in their meetings to see what they do. Learn from them, and implement what you learn.

- You can take the best sales rep in your company out to lunch and pick that person's brain.

- You can invest in yourself and hire a coach to work with you to help you improve. Perhaps I can be of assistance? You can reach out to me via email: eric@thegoalguide.com.

- You can enroll yourself in a sales seminar to learn more skills.

- You can also turn your car into a mobile classroom and listen to audiobooks about sales while you're driving.

The point is that your success is in your hands. No matter what you've accomplished so far, you can do so much more. Your potential is unlimited, and I truly believe in you. Being in sales is one of the most rewarding careers you could have chosen. You get to help people solve problems and achieve goals that they may not know how to achieve until you come along. Being in sales comes with a lot of work, rejection, and at times pain. However, it also comes with many rewards, victories, successes, and personal growth.

I applaud you for choosing sales as your career and thank you for investing your time to read this book. I wish you the best of luck on your journey and hope that you not only take the lessons from this book for yourself but also pass them along to others who are striving to improve!

Made in the USA
Middletown, DE
03 June 2023

31767085R00106